W9-CAV-802

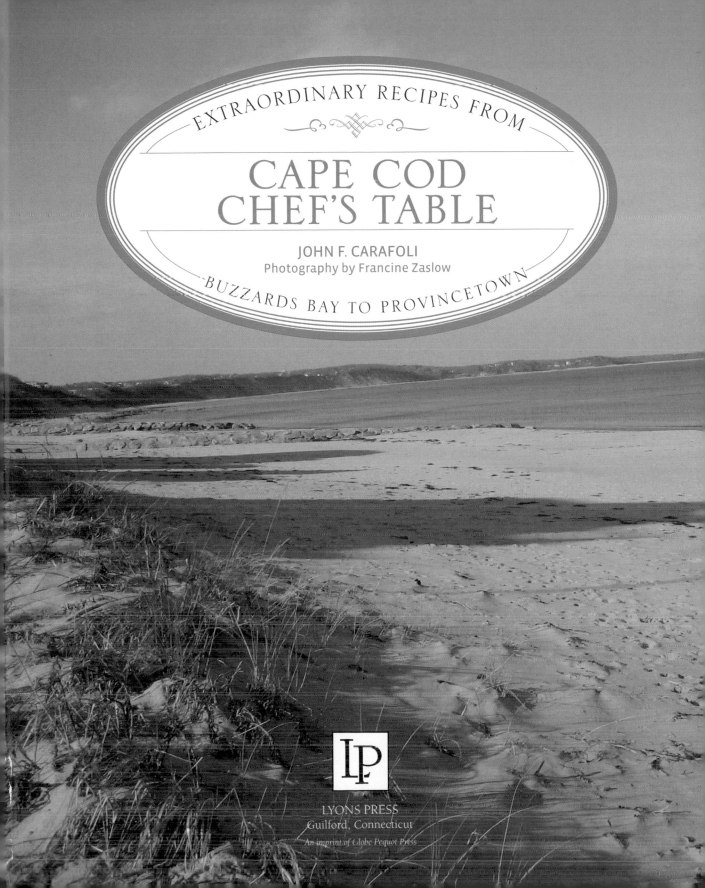

EXTRAORDINARY RECIPES FROM

CAPE COD
CHEF'S TABLE

JOHN F. CARAFOLI

Photography by Francine Zaslow

BUZZARDS BAY TO PROVINCETOWN

LP

LYONS PRESS
Guilford, Connecticut
An imprint of Globe Pequot Press

To buy books in quantity for corporate use or incentives, call **(800) 962–0973** or e-mail **premiums@GlobePequot.com.**

Lyons Press is an imprint of Globe Pequot Press.

All photography by Francine Zaslow except pages i, 80–81, and 138 courtesy of the author and those otherwise noted.

Editor: Amy Lyons
Project Editor: Tracee Williams
Text Design: Libby Kingsbury
Layout Artist: Nancy Freeborn
Map: Alena Joy Pearce © Morris Book Publishing, LLC

Library of Congress Cataloging-in-Publication Data

Carafoli, John F.
 Cape Cod chef's table : extraordinary recipes from Buzzards Bay to Provincetown / John F. Carafoli ; photography by Francine Zaslow.
     pages cm
 Summary: "Over the past several years, Cape Cod's culinary landscape has evolved. The huge resurgence and interest in organic and local farming has also reached the Cape, and chefs here are connecting with farmers and growers. Today's Cape presents a thriving and unique culinary landscape and Cape Cod Chef's Table gives readers, locals, and visitors a new perspective on this culinary scene. Featuring recipes for the home cook from the Cape's celebrated eateries and purveyors along with full-color photos." — Provided by publisher.
 ISBN 978-0-7627-8636-7 (hardback)
1. Cooking, American—New England style. 2. Cooking—Massachusetts—Cape Cod. I. Title.
 TX715.2.N48C37 2013
 641.5974—dc23

                                                                          2013010259

Printed in the United States of America

10 9 8 7 6 5 4 3 2 1

Restaurants and chefs often come and go, and menus are ever-changing. We recommend you call ahead to obtain current information before visiting any of the establishments in this book.

For John. He sings, and I cook.

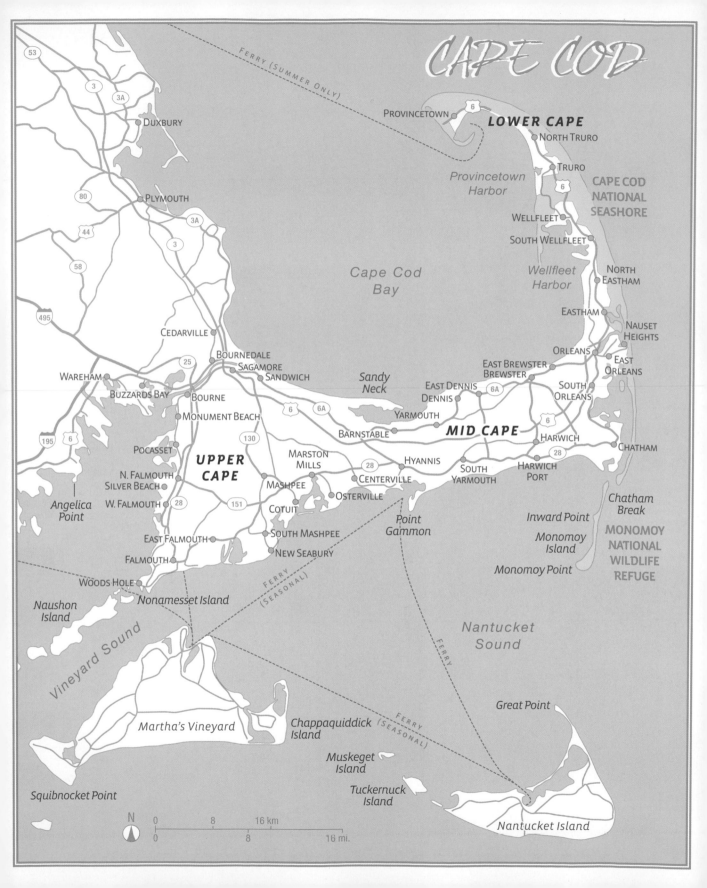

CONTENTS

PHOTO BY DEB JOHNSON

Acknowledgments

I had a book proposal for an Italian/American cookbook. It was the story of the immigrants who came to Sagamore in the late 1800s, their stories, traditions, and recipes. A friend, a cookbook author herself, suggested I send it to Globe Pequot Press. As I was typing my letter introducing the project, and myself, an e-mail came in. It was from Amy Lyons, Editorial Director, Travel and Local Cooking, Globe Pequot Press, saying she was looking for a writer and photographer to do a book called the *Cape Cod Chef's Table* and thought I would be a good fit. It was a bizarre coincidence, one of those circumstances in life one cannot explain. I was looking for an interesting new project, and here it was. Now that the book is done, I would like to thank Amy Lyons for choosing me to write this book. Amy allowed me to fly with my creative ideas and concepts.

I would also like to thank several people who worked with me to produce this book. I could not have done this project without their help.

Thanks to my talented, creative photographer Francine Zaslow. Francine is primarily a studio photographer, and we go back several years. On countless commercial and editorial food shoots, I styled the food and she photographed it. Francine also photographed the cover for the third edition of my book *Food Photography and Styling*. This project took her from the comfort zone of her bright, sunny studio on an adventurous road trip. I took her places she never thought she would go. Like knee-deep into the cold water of the ocean, photographing fishermen unloading lobsters from a boat on a brutally cold, windy day. Or forced to attend an oyster festival in the pouring rain. Often Deb Johnson, Francine's wonderfully efficient studio producer, or photo assistant Cody O'longhlin would join us. And while we were on the road, digital tech Dan Klempa prepared the beautiful photos we were shooting for publication.

Every writer needs a second pair of eyes, and a special thanks goes to my professional proofreader and "food lover" Deborah Karacozian. When we have worked together on projects in the past, we collaborated over the phone and by computer. We never met until this project.

As in most chef's cookbooks, recipes can be problematic. Sometimes it's because the amounts of the ingredients in a recipe need to be scaled down, or sometimes the recipe is just too complicated for a home cook to do. I needed someone knowledgeable to format and sometimes test the recipes, to make sure they were consistent throughout the book. I found Nancy Boyson through a colleague of mine. Thank you, Nancy, you helped make my project move faster.

Good food deserves good wine, so special thanks to my special friends at Town Wine & Spirits in Eastham—Leslie Plumb, my "wine goddess," for her exciting descriptions and unusual wine pairings for each recipe, and Kevin Plumb for his technical support when I needed it. I also want to thank Paul Opacki at Maypop Antiques for letting me use many of his unusual antiques for this book and other projects.

And, of course, this book would not be possible without the many chefs and owners of the restaurants, specialty shops, and eateries who generously opened their kitchens to let me sample their recipes and food. Thank you.

Introduction

I grew up in the town of Bourne in the predominately Italian village of Sagamore, where my grandparents had settled after emigrating from Northern Italy. It was a simpler life back then. My family and I bought free-range chickens (and fresh eggs) from Joe Rigazio's farm on the other side of the bridge, and milk and cream were delivered to our doorstep from Roberti's Dairy in Sandwich. Most people had gardens in their backyards and grew their own grapes for making wine. I picked blueberries in the woods and sold them for carnival money (half went in my bucket, the other half went in my mouth). There wasn't much in terms of a restaurant scene. On Friday nights my dad would bring home lobsters from the marina, which my mom would boil. I wouldn't eat them because I didn't like lobster or fish. But one of my favorite food memories involves lobster. My great-uncle was a professional chef in Connecticut. When jovial "Zio" visited my family, he'd make a variety of cacciatore-style dishes, and the one still vivid in my mind was lobster combined with a delicious rich tomato sauce. I would avoid eating any lobster, but I used to dunk a piece of our local "horn" bread into the rich sauce, relishing the complex flavors without realizing I was tasting traces of lobster.

Food prepared by my grandmother was very important to our household, as it was for the Italian immigrant mothers in our neighborhood. Over the years I've written about the instinctive knowledge and wisdom they had about food and cooking. My passion for these highly skilled women in the Italian Sagamore area led me to want to document their wisdom and recipes.

I left Cape Cod to go to art school in Boston, and then I moved to Chicago to pursue a career in the art and design world. My childhood love of food and cooking continued to be a large part of my life. I eventually moved back to the Cape. Here I re-created my life as a food stylist and author. I now live about ten miles from where I grew up, in an 1840s farmhouse on more than an acre of land. In some ways life is the way it was when I was growing up: I have chickens for fresh eggs and eight assorted fruit trees, and I still pick blueberries from the bushes in my own yard. All season long I go clamming, and in November, when oyster season starts, you'll find me on the flats. Today lobster is one of my favorite foods.

Like most things in life, change is inevitable. The small friendly community of Sagamore that I knew as a child is quite different today. Many of the women who showed me how to make special Italian dishes and gave me their recipes have passed on, along with their loving traditions. But one of the most important changes taking place on the Cape became very obvious once I was living here. As in many parts of the United States, the idea of "buy local, eat local" was taking off. Today the farm-to-table movement on the Cape has become firmly established and local and organic are words you hear all the time.

From early spring to late fall, I see chefs working with local farmers and purveyors to get the freshest possible products. However, one real difficulty on the Cape is our short growing season. To compensate, some farmers have greenhouses and extend the

season by growing indoors. Some Cape farmers are also starting to produce their own pork and lamb.

The emphasis on sustainable fishing cannot be denied. As the fishing industry has changed, aquaculture has grown. Many people have oyster grants, and an aquaponic farm grows hypotonic vegetables and fish in a recycling system. Oyster farming has also expanded, and you can now find Cape Cod oysters from here to New York.

In addition, a number of cottage industries around food and food products have sprung up around the Cape. Small companies and individuals are making and selling a variety of products such as jams, jellies, breads, and textiles.

All of this is to say that today you can find more and more people living off the land and making a living with what is available to them on Cape Cod And this is helping Cape Cod become a food destination as well as a popular tourist spot.

Cape Cod is more than just fun clam shacks offering fried clams and clam chowder. Yes, there are many good ones, but today there is so much more. There is a new energy in the restaurant and food world on the Cape. European chefs are moving here and starting their own restaurants. You can now find Italian, Brazilian, Mexican, and French restaurants, but there is always that touch of Cape Cod cultural DNA in each restaurant, fresh and local. Chefs are reinventing some of the old New England classics. For example, one chef has updated the traditional clam chowder by replacing white potatoes with sweet potatoes. Another adds lobster to the classic Benedict; instead of the classic cheesecake, lavender and goat cheese are added.

Some of the chefs' dishes included in this book may seem complicated at first, including Twenty-Eight Atlantic Chef James Hackney's Caramelized Scallops. This is really a number of recipes within one. Instead of making the entire recipe, however, you could make the pea puree for one dish, or use his gnocchi recipe for a first course with a light marinara sauce or just a sage butter.

This book follows the same road a visitor would take when visiting the Cape. Everyone goes over the Sagamore or Bourne Bridge and travels down Route 6 or turns off to Route 28 or Route 6A. The book does the same thing. It winds through the fifteen towns and their respective villages to explore each town and its environment through a new lens. I talked to chefs about the food they serve and where they get their produce and products. I attended the annual scallop and oyster festivals, and I tasted many of the products the local cottage industries have to offer.

I have tried to make this more than just a cookbook by adding my own remembrances, thoughts, and experiences about the Cape as it was in the past and is today. This is my Cape Cod, the place where I have a picnic after a day at the beach and celebrate special occasions with friends and family with dinner at home or at one of these fine restaurants. Join me for this food journey along the Cape—it will be fun, with a variety of fresh, local delicious food!

UPPER CAPE

Añejo Mexican Bistro & Tequila Bar

188 Main Street
Falmouth, MA 02540
(508) 388-7631
anejomexicanbistro.com
Owners: Jesse Kersey and Jamie Surprenant
Chef: Josh Hanoka

Since August 2010, Añejo has been a bustling establishment on Main Street in Falmouth, a surprising taste of Mexico in this fairly traditional town. The owners are Jesse Kersey and Jamie Surprenant. Jesse grew up in the San Francisco area, and Jamie was raised on Cape Cod and worked in his family's restaurant for two decades. He is also a co-owner of the successful Five Bays Bistro in Osterville. Chef Josh Hanoka is from San Jose and got involved when the owners first came up with the idea of opening a Mexican restaurant in Falmouth. "This has been a great experience for me because I was involved at the beginning. We had similar ideas and concepts for what a Mexican bistro should be," says Josh.

The bar has over sixty-five different brands of tequila to choose from, ranging from Bianco (silver) and Reposado (aged), to the Añejo (extra-aged). The menu runs the gamut. Choose from the freshly made tableside Guacamole in an authentic molcajete served with plenty of fresh, crisp tortillas to house specials like the recipe shown here.

Guacamole

(SERVES 4)

4 Hass ripe avocados, halved, pitted, and peeled
½ white sweet onion, peeled and finely chopped
½ bunch fresh cilantro, finely chopped
1 jalapeño, stemmed, seeded, and finely chopped
2 tablespoons fresh lime juice (from 1 lime)
Cotija cheese, for garnish

Smash avocados to desired consistency. Add remaining ingredients and mix well. Transfer to a serving bowl and press a sheet of plastic wrap directly against the surface of the guacamole until ready to serve. Remove plastic wrap and sprinkle with cotija cheese before serving.

Serve with tortilla chips and a margarita.

Pescado Encornflecado

(SERVES 6)

For the salsa verde:

1 pound (11–12) fresh tomatillos, husked,
    washed, and cut into chunks
2 cups chicken broth
2 jalapeños or 3 serrano chiles, stemmed,
    cut in half, and seeded
1 tablespoon vegetable oil
1 small yellow onion, peeled and chopped
1 garlic clove, peeled and chopped
2 tablespoons chopped fresh cilantro
Salt to taste

For the rice:

2 cups water
1 cup long-grain Basmati rice
1 tablespoon butter

For the cod:

½ cup all-purpose flour
1 teaspoon salt
2 large eggs
3 tablespoons water
6 cups crushed cornflakes
6 (5–6 ounce) skinless cod fillets, about ¾-inch thick
¼ cup corn oil, more if needed, for each fillet

For the corn:

6 ears fresh corn, shucked and silks removed
6 tablespoons mayonnaise
¾ teaspoon cayenne pepper or chili powder
4–6 tablespoons finely shredded cotija or
    Parmesan cheese

To assemble the dish:

½ cup chopped fresh cilantro
2 tablespoons fresh lime juice (from 1 lime)
1 teaspoon grated lime zest
1 cup cotija cheese, grated
1–2 limes, cut into wedges

For the salsa verde: Place tomatillos, chicken broth, and chiles in a saucepan and bring to a boil. Cook until vegetables are fairly soft, about 5 to 10 minutes. Meanwhile, heat the oil in a sauté pan and add the onion. Cook, stirring occasionally, until softened, about 5 minutes. Add the garlic and cook 1 minute more. Stir in the boiled tomatillos and chiles and remove from heat. Transfer to a food processor, along with the cilantro and salt to taste. Blend until smooth. Set aside.

For the rice: Bring water to boil in a medium-size saucepan with a lid. Stir in the rice and butter. Cover the pan, reduce heat to low, and simmer until rice is tender and water is absorbed, about 20 minutes. Set aside and keep warm.

For the cod: Preheat oven to 350°F. Set up three shallow dishes to make a breading station. Place the flour in the first dish and mix in ½ teaspoon salt. Combine the eggs, water, and ½ teaspoon salt in the second dish and beat with a fork until well blended. Place the cornflakes in the third dish. Dredge each fillet in flour, shaking off any excess; turn the fish in the beaten egg; and then transfer the fish to the cornflakes, pressing firmly to thoroughly coat on all sides. Place coated fillets on a plate in a single layer without touching, as they are breaded. Heat the oil in a sauté pan and lightly brown each fillet. Transfer to a baking sheet and bake until just cooked through, about 8 minutes.

For the corn: Preheat the grill to medium-high and grill the corn, turning occasionally, until lightly charred, about 8 to 10 minutes. Transfer to a platter. Quickly spread the corn with mayonnaise and then roll in the cheese. Sprinkle a small amount of cayenne or chili powder on each ear.

To assemble the dish: At serving time, stir the cilantro, lime juice, and zest into the rice. Mound some rice on each dinner plate and arrange fish fillets on top. Spoon salsa verde over the fish. Complete each plate with an ear of corn, a sprinkle of cotija cheese, and a lime wedge.

BELFRY INNE & BISTRO

8 JARVES STREET
SANDWICH, MA 02563
(508) 888-8550
BELFRYINN.COM
OWNER: CHRISTOPHER WILSON
EXECUTIVE CHEF: BENJAMIN PORTER

Between 1995 and 2003, Christopher Wilson purchased and renovated three run-down buildings on Jarves Street in the heart of the village of Sandwich. These three buildings—a Victorian building known as "the Painted Lady," a deconsecrated Roman Catholic Church, and a federal-style building that once housed the company that built the Cape Cod Canal—were renovated and transformed into the Belfry Inne & Bistro.

The Bistro is in the church, which is now known as the Abbey. Wilson used ingenuity and imagination as he salvaged and reused as much of the original church as possible. The one-time confessional is now the wine cellar, and many of the pews have been put to different uses. Some became the bar, some were used as paneling for the walls, and some became beds. Still in their original homes, however, are most of the stained-glass windows, and the grand fireplace is now the focal point of the main dining room.

The food served in this architectural marvel is some of the best you will find on the Upper Cape. Chef Benjamin Porter graduated from Johnson & Wales University and went to work in California, where he learned the importance of sourcing and preparing fresh local ingredients. His specialty is contemporary American seasonal cuisine. The menu is varied, with tasting plates, lighter fare, and gluten-free offerings. You can have Cape Littlenecks in chowder or baked and stuffed. For entrees there's Dayboat Chatham Codfish, Seared Local Sea Scallops, and Atlantic Halibut.

You can eat at the bar, dine in the main room, or, in warmer weather, sit outside on the patio. There's a wine tasting every Wednesday evening, and the Bistro does catering for special events and weddings. Treat yourself to a dining experience here. The combination of extraordinary surroundings and wonderful food is heavenly.

Pan-Seared Atlantic Halibut

(SERVES 4)

For the beurre blanc:

4 ounces pancetta, diced

1 cup dry white wine

1 small shallot, peeled and diced

4 sprigs fresh lemon thyme

1 bay leaf

½ cup (4 ounces) cold unsalted butter, diced

For the succotash:

4 ears fresh sweet corn, shucked and silks removed

1 pint cherry tomatoes, washed, stemmed, and
  quartered

4 ounces shelled edamame

½ small red onion, peeled and diced

1 red bell pepper, roasted, seeded, and diced

For the halibut:

4 (8-ounce) Atlantic halibut skinless fillets

Salt and pepper to taste

3 tablespoons extra-virgin olive oil

For the buerre blanc: Place pancetta in a sauté pan over medium-low heat and cook, stirring occasionally, until the fat has rendered and meat is lightly browned. With a slotted spoon, transfer pancetta to paper towels to drain. Reserve 2 tablespoons fat in the pan and set aside.

While the pancetta is cooking, combine the white wine, shallot, thyme, and bay leaf in a small saucepan and boil until the wine is reduced to ¼ cup. Strain and return the wine to the pan over low heat, discarding the herbs. Gradually whisk in the cold butter, a little at a time, to create an emulsified sauce. Stir in the pancetta; keep warm until serving time.

For the succotash: Grill the corn over medium-high heat, turning occasionally, until done, 8 to 10 minutes. Cut the kernels off the cobs; there should be about 2 cups. Return the sauté pan with the pancetta fat to medium heat. Add the corn, tomatoes, edamame, and onion and sauté until onions are translucent, about 5 minutes. Stir in the roasted pepper and set aside.

For the halibut: Preheat oven to 375°F. Season the fish with salt and pepper. Heat the oil in a large ovenproof sauté pan and add the fish. Cook until undersides are browned and move easily in the pan, about 3 minutes; turn fish over and place the pan in the oven to finish cooking, about 8 minutes more, depending on the thickness of the fish.

To assemble the dish: Reheat the succotash if necessary and divide it among four plates. Position the fish on top and spoon the beurre blanc over the fish.

WINE SUGGESTION:

Pinot Nero Bianco. This bright and vibrant Italian white wine has a pale copper color. It's a full-bodied and racy bottle of absolute joy made from the red grape Pinot Noir. A most unusual find, it's ideal to serve with pan-seared halibut

Bleu

10 Market Street
Mashpee Commons
Mashpee, MA 02649
(508) 539-7907
bleurestaurant.com
Chef/Owner: Frederic Feufeu

Mashpee Commons is an open-air shopping mall created to look like a New England town center. On the way to New Seabury and Falmouth, it's a good place to stop for a little shopping, an ice cream cone, or a lovely French meal. Chef Frederick Feufeu, a native of the Loire Valley, went to the celebrated Les Sorbets School in Brittany. He spent some time in Paris and London and eventually found himself working at some of the best restaurants in New York City, including the Rainbow Room and the Brasserie Pascal.

After marriage and children, Chef Feufeu and his wife decided to make a change. He had always thought of having his own restaurant, and because he had a connection to Cape Cod, it seemed a likely place to do it.

Chef Feufeu opened his bistro in 2003, and his fine cooking has become a year-round staple in the Mashpee area. The comfortable room with its understated simple decor complements his French style of cooking. The waitstaff is friendly, attentive, and knowledgeable. In warmer months there is outdoor seating, but during the winter months, it is a cozy comfortable place for a quiet French dinner for any occasion. You'll find Chef Feufeu's classic French touch in dishes like the Escargot de Bourgogne Farcis and the French Onion Soup. There is plenty of fresh fish prepared in a variety of different ways on the menu, along with steaks, lamb, and chicken. On special days of the week, try the special three-course prix fixe menu.

ESCARGOTS WITH GARLIC BUTTER

(SERVES 6)

For the garlic butter:

2 cups (1 pound) unsalted butter, softened
1 cup chopped fresh curly parsley
¼ cup Pernod
10 garlic cloves, minced
2 tablespoons chopped fresh thyme
1 teaspoon fine sea salt

1 (16-ounce) can escargots, rinsed and drained well,
   with shells if desired
Crusty French bread, for serving

For the garlic butter: Combine the butter, parsley, Pernod, garlic, thyme, and salt in a bowl and mix until thoroughly blended. Garlic butter can be prepared ahead; cover and refrigerate. Bring to room temperature before using.

To assemble the dish: Preheat oven to 400°F. Bring a pot of water to boil. Add the escargots, cook 2 minutes, then drain and rinse with cold water to stop the cooking. If using shells, stuff each shell generously with garlic butter, add an escargot, top with more butter, and place in a gratin dish. (Unbaked escargots can be refrigerated, tightly covered, for up to 1 week.) Bake until hot and bubbly, about 7 minutes. Serve immediately with crusty French bread.

WINE SUGGESTION:
Red Burgundy. French red Burgundy is made entirely from Pinot Noir and it's a natural accompaniment for Escargot. Pairing regional food with regional wine is easy peasy. An earthy and downright sexy choice to wash down those snails!

Onion Soup Gratinée

(SERVES 6)

¼ cup olive oil

1 tablespoon unsalted butter

4 large onions, peeled and sliced ¼ inch thick

2 cups dry red wine

2–3 sprigs fresh thyme

1 garlic clove, minced

1 bay leaf

6 cups chicken stock

2 cups rich beef stock

To assemble the dish:

12 stale baguette slices

2 cups (16 ounces) grated Gruyère cheese

Heat the oil and butter together in a large heavy pot over medium heat. Turn the heat up to medium-high and then add the onions and sauté, stirring and turning frequently, until they are dark brown and very soft, about 30 minutes. Turn the heat to high and add the wine, thyme, garlic, and bay leaf. Cook, scraping up any browned bits stuck to the pan, until wine has reduced by half, about 10 minutes. Add the chicken and beef stocks and bring to a boil. Adjust heat to a simmer and cook about 45 minutes.

Preheat broiler or oven to 400°F. Arrange six individual soup crocks or ovenproof bowls on a sturdy baking sheet. Remove thyme sprigs and bay leaf and ladle the soup into the bowls. Fit two baguette slices on top of each and cover with a generous amount of cheese. Bake until cheese melts to a crispy brown, about 3 minutes.

WINE SUGGESTION:
Cru Beaujolais. A French cru Beaujolais made entirely from the Gamay grape which is vinified in the elegant style of Pinot Noir is a fantastic choice for onion soup. The bright cherry and raspberry notes balance the sweetness of the onions, while the underlying granitic minerality complements the soup's somewhat rustic nature. An excellent choice for a crisp Autumn evening.

THE BROWN JUG

155 MAIN STREET
SANDWICH, MA 02563
(508) 888-4669
THEBROWNJUG.COM
OWNER: MICHAEL JOHNSTON

Like most of the buildings in Sandwich, the two buildings that Michael Johnston owns have had many incarnations. In the 1920s the building on Main Street was a grocery store and then a diner. The building on Jarves Street dates back to 1873, when it was a shoe and boot store and in later years a meeting hall for Civil War veterans. Some time after that it became a dry goods store called Butters. But now the corner of Main and Jarves is home to the Brown Jug.

The Brown Jug opened on Main Street in the fall of 2003, offering specialty foods, ceramics, and linens from around the world. The wine room opened the

following spring around the corner on Jarves Street, and by 2009 the Brown Jug had expanded to include a cafe as well as a cappuccino and latte bar. It is one of the best places on the Cape to buy wonderful cheeses and wines, enjoy a cocktail or a glass of wine with lunch on the outdoor patio, or even have a party catered.

Johnston traveled widely before settling down in Sandwich. "My mother was in the restaurant business, so I grew up with it," he says. "I went to school in England and then in Canada and worked in the food, beverage, and hospitality business. I worked at the Four Seasons hotel in Boston, then bought a home here in Sandwich." Michael emphasizes the importance of good communication with his patrons. "Customers will come in and tell me that they are having a party or special gathering for twenty people and want something special for the occasion. I first ask for

a few guidelines, such as how many people, what is the price line, what are you comfortable with. I am totally comfortable with their needs. Then the fun begins for me! I do best when my customers let me create something within their needs."

Café Chew

4 Merchant's Road
Sandwich, MA 02563
(508) 888-7717
cafechew.com
Owners: Chef Bob King and Tobin Wirt

In its short existence Café Chew has won numerous accolades. Top ten coffeehouse, best lunch, best brunch, best breakfast sandwich, and the raves keep coming. Proud to be "organic, natural, whole," Café Chew is a place where you'll feel at home having coffee or a sandwich, surrounded by friendly faces and an attentive staff. The walls are Tuscan orange, and each table is beautifully hand painted with images from napkins that owners Bob King and Tobin Wirt brought back from Provence. Artist Chris Reverdy painted the tables. She was opening the Brush Studio and Gallery next door at the same time King and Wirt were opening the cafe. It was a natural fit. In warmer months have a seat at the outdoor patio and enjoy the beautiful flower garden.

King and Wirt were no strangers to the food industry when they opened Café Chew. "We both have been in the restaurant business for twenty-five years," says King. "We got burnt out, took some time off, and went to work for other people. This definitely did not work for us. We started looking around at what was happening and working in the restaurant world in this economic down turn. Who is doing well? Pain D'Avignon had a great bread shop in Hyannis. We live in Sandwich. Why not open a sandwich shop and serve breakfast and lunch? We have been here for three years now, and it is very successful."

Café Chew's breakfast and lunch menu is extensive. For breakfast there's organic coffee, lattes, and cappuccinos and organic steel-cut oats with cinnamon–brown sugar and toasted nuts and raisins, as well as a smoked salmon platter and fresh fruit. Lunch consists of specialty salads, sandwiches, and a showcase of desserts. "We use Pain D'Avignon's sourdough, multi-grain, and of course cranberry nut bread. We buy our honey from E&T Farms, in West Barnstable," explains King. Café Chew uses produce purchased locally from individual farmers and Crow Farm in East Sandwich.

The "Pilgrim"

(SERVES 2)

This is one of the Café Chew's signature sandwiches, made with Pain D'Avignon's Cranberry Walnut Bread. Use freshly roasted turkey breast or leftovers from a turkey dinner.

For the herb bread stuffing:

½ cup (4 ounces) unsalted butter
3 celery stalks, trimmed and diced
1 onion, peeled and diced
4 cups crumbled white or wheat bread, day old or
    lightly toasted
1 tablespoon Bell's seasoning or ground sage
Salt and pepper to taste
¼–½ cup water or turkey stock

For the cranberry mayonnaise:

¾ cup whole cranberry sauce
¾ cup mayonnaise

To assemble the dish:

4 slices your favorite nut bread
4–6 slices roasted turkey breast
4 romaine lettuce leaves, washed and dried

For the herb bread stuffing: Melt the butter in a sauté pan over medium-high heat. Add the celery and onion and cook until the onion is golden and translucent, about 5 minutes. Add the bread, seasoning, and salt and pepper to taste. Moisten with enough water or stock to just bring stuffing together.

For the cranberry mayonnaise: Place the cranberry sauce and mayonnaise in a blender and process until well combined.

To assemble the two sandwiches: Pile stuffing on one slice of nut bread, and top with turkey and romaine. Spread cranberry mayo on the other slice of bread and place it on top of the lettuce. Cut in half and serve immediately with a frothy cold glass of Cape Cod Beer (page 72).

The Chart Room

1 Shipyard Lane
Cataumet, MA 02534
(508) 563-5350
chartroomcataumet.com
Owners: David Jarvis and Tom Gordon
Chef: Tom Gordon

The Chart Room is a seasonal restaurant with rustic Cape Cod charm. It is casual and fun and has great fresh seafood. It is open for lunch or dinner, and you can choose to eat outside on the lawn or inside at either the long bar or an individual table. All seats have a great view of the harbor. Some evenings have lively entertainment, but almost all evenings have beautiful, breathtaking sunsets.

David Jarvis runs the front of the house and the bar while Chef Tom Gordon runs the kitchen. They have been business partners for over forty years. Both are native New Englanders.

"This business started with my parents and their friends Gordon Swanson—Swannie as we called him—and his wife," says Jarvis. Tom Gordon started in the kitchen as a dishwasher under Swannie and says, "The biggest sellers on our menu are the baked stuffed lobsters, the lobster salad sandwich, and the swordfish."

The interior of the restaurant is covered with memorabilia and history. Jarvis points to various signs on the walls of the restaurant. "People actually bring me things to pin up. Over there is a sign from Swift's Market, in Osterville; another sign was given to us by a gentleman who retired his boat and wanted the sign to be hung here. There have been years and years of people bringing me signs to put up."

STEAMED MUSSELS

(SERVES 4)

½ cup olive oil
¼ cup chopped garlic
2–3 sprigs fresh thyme
1–2 bay leaves
4 pounds mussels, scrubbed and beards removed
1 cup white wine
¼ cup water
Parsley for garnish

Combine the olive oil, garlic, thyme, and bay leaves in a large Dutch oven or other pot with a lid. Sauté over medium heat 5 minutes, stirring occasionally; be careful not to burn the garlic. Add the mussels and raise the heat to high; add the wine and water and mix well. Cover and cook, shaking the pot a few times, until the mussels open, about 10 minutes. Discard any mussels that do not open. Divide mussels, along with the cooking liquid, among 4 bowls and garnish with parsley.

Baked Stuffed Lobster

(SERVES 2)

For the bread crumbs:

1–1½ cups fine dry bread crumbs
¼ teaspoon garlic powder
¼ teaspoon onion powder
¼ teaspoon dried parsley flakes
¼ teaspoon paprika
¼ teaspoon white pepper
3–4 tablespoons unsalted butter, melted

To assemble the dish:

2 (1½–pound) live lobsters
10–12 ounces freshly cooked lobster meat
½ cup unsalted butter, melted

For the bread crumbs: Place bread crumbs in a bowl and add the spices; mix well. Add just enough melted butter to evenly moisten; set aside.

To assemble the dish: Preheat oven to 450°F. Place the lobsters cut side up on a baking sheet and loosely stuff cavities with lobster meat. Drizzle the meat with melted butter, top with seasoned bread crumbs, and cover each stuffed cavity with a small piece of foil to prevent burning. Bake until golden brown, about 15 to 20 minutes.

WINE SUGGESTION:
White Burgundy. A full-bodied French white Burgundy made from 100 percent Chardonnay has wonderful structure along with ripe fruit, displaying undertones of lively minerality with a crisp citrus palate. Lobsters and mussels with a Saint Veran? Yes, please!

HOW TO EAT (OR DEAL WITH) A COOKED LOBSTER

1. Twist off the claws.

2. Crack each claw with a nutcracker.

3. Separate the tailpiece from the body by arching its back until it cracks.

4. Remove the meat from the tail by holding it in your hand and squeezing to break the shell. Grasping both sides of the tail, use thumbs to separate the tail and remove the meat.

5. Unhinge the back from the body. The body contains the "tomalley" or liver of the lobster. This turns green when cooked. Many people consider this one of the best parts of the lobster. If it is a female lobster, you might find the bright red "coral," or eggs, a real delicacy.

6. Open the remaining part of the body by cracking it apart sideways. There is some good meat in this section of the body.

Cranberry's Restaurant and Pub

618 MacArthur Boulevard
Pocasset, MA 02559
(508) 392-9620
CRANBERRYSRESTAURANT.COM
Owners: Marc and Bree Swierkowski
Executive Chef: Marc Swierkowski
General Manager: Bree Kwiatkowski

I first met Marc and Bree Swierkowski while sitting at the bar at Ella's Wood Burning Oven in Wareham, a small town on the other side of the Cape Cod Canal. Next to me was a young couple, and we struck up a conversation. It turned out that they were the owners of Ella's and were on a "busman's holiday." They worked at Marc's other restaurant in Pocasset, a place called Cranberry's Restaurant and Pub. As we talked, they described some of the dishes, and within a few days I was dining at Cranberry's.

From the street the restaurant looks unassuming, but inside the atmosphere is comfortable and casual. Marc is a wonderful chef, and his food never disappoints. I tried one of the dishes we had discussed, the Buttermilk Fried Chicken. Delicious. I asked Marc about what inspires him. "When I have an opportunity to travel to a new region, I am inspired by the culture and local chefs. Many times there's a new ingredient that I haven't used before, or not for a very long time, that is available through a purveyor or a farmers' market," he says. "As this industry grows, we as chefs need to grow and run with the trends but still keep the integrity of the dish. With so many ingredients and so many chefs, the thing that I believe distinguishes us is quality, and knowing the authentic techniques of cooking." Chef Swierkowski's food is some of the best on the Upper Cape.

Buttermilk Fried Chicken

(SERVES 4–6)

For the brine:

1 gallon water
1 cup kosher salt
½ cup sugar
8 bay leaves
2 cinnamon sticks
2 tablespoons whole black peppercorns
5 allspice berries
5 whole cloves
2½ pounds all natural chicken, preferably 2 breasts,
   2 drumsticks, and 2 thighs

For the watermelon salad:

¼ seedless watermelon, rind removed and flesh
   cut in cubes
1½ cups fresh corn kernels (from 3 ears sweet corn)
1 pint cherry tomatoes, washed, dried, and quartered
1 small red onion, peeled and diced
2 jalapeños, stemmed, seeded, and diced
2 limes, zested and juiced
¼ cup thinly sliced fresh mint leaves
¼ cup honey
¼ cup extra-virgin olive oil

For the fried chicken:

2 cups all-purpose flour
2 tablespoons onion powder
2 tablespoons garlic powder
2 tablespoons smoked paprika
1 teaspoon cayenne pepper
1 tablespoon kosher salt
2 teaspoons cracked black pepper
2 cups buttermilk
Vegetable, canola, or peanut oil for frying

To assemble the dish:

¼ cup honey
Coarse sea salt

For the brine: Combine brine ingredients in a large pot over high heat, stirring to dissolve the salt and sugar. Bring to a boil, then adjust the heat to a simmer and cook 5 minutes. Remove from heat and chill thoroughly. Place chicken in the brine; refrigerate for 12 to 24 hours.

For the watermelon salad: Combine the salad ingredients in a bowl and toss gently to combine. Can be prepared a day ahead; cover and refrigerate until serving.

For the fried chicken: Combine the flour, onion powder, garlic powder, paprika, cayenne, salt, and cracked pepper in a large shallow bowl and mix well. Place the buttermilk in another shallow bowl and set aside. Fill a Dutch oven or large cast iron skillet halfway with oil and place over medium-high heat. Attach a candy thermometer to the pan and heat the oil to 350°F.

While the oil is heating, coat the chicken: Working with one piece at a time, roll the chicken in the flour mixture, shaking off any excess, then dip in buttermilk to coat completely. Return the chicken to the flour, rolling and turning to make sure there are no bare spots. Leave the chicken in the flour for a few minutes, then roll it to coat again. Transfer the pieces to a wire rack as they are done, making sure coated pieces do not touch.

Carefully add the chicken to the hot oil and fry for 10 to 13 minutes, until the internal temperature of a thigh reaches 155°F on an instant-read thermometer. Drain the cooked chicken on paper towels, then transfer to a clean wire rack to rest in a warm place for 5 minutes before serving. (This will allow the chicken to reach its proper serving temperature.) If the chicken gets cold, reheat in a 375°F oven.

To assemble the dish: Place a large spoonful of watermelon salad on each plate. Arrange the fried chicken beside it and garnish the chicken with a drizzle of honey and a sprinkle of salt. Serve immediately.

WINE SUGGESTION:
Australian Semillon. Sometimes when you have a rich dish like fried chicken, it's nice to provide contrast with a refreshingly crisp and acidic white wine. A Semillon from Hunter Valley in Australia has classic lemongrass and straw aromas along with apple blossom and lime notes and striking acidic structure to cut through the richness of the chicken.

Fresh Littleneck Clam Chowder

(SERVES 4–6)

8 tablespoons (4 ounces) unsalted butter, divided

3 slices thick-cut bacon, diced

½ cup chopped onions

⅓ cup chopped celery

2 bay leaves

2 cups sea clam juice

½ cup peeled and grated russet potato

¼ cup peeled and grated sweet potato

1 cup heavy cream

12–16 littleneck clams, shells scrubbed of sand

1 (6-ounce) sweet potato, peeled and diced

1 tablespoon chopped fresh thyme

8 dashes Tabasco sauce

Salt and pepper to taste

Combine 4 tablespoons butter and the bacon in a heavy-bottomed 4-quart pot over medium-low heat. Cook until the butter is melted and the bacon is crisp, stirring often.

Raise the heat to medium-high and add the onions, celery, and bay leaves; sauté until onion is translucent, about 5 minutes.

Add the clam juice and bring to a boil. Adjust the heat and simmer for 10 minutes to blend flavors.

Add the grated potatoes, stirring constantly, until potatoes are softened and chowder starts to thicken, about 8 to 10 minutes. Remove the pan from the heat, take out the bay leaves, and use an immersion blender to puree the chowder base.

Return the chowder to the pot. Stir in the cream and return the pot to medium-high heat. Bring to a boil, stirring often.

Add the clams, diced sweet potato, remaining 4 tablespoons butter, thyme, and Tabasco; return to a simmer and cook, stirring often, just until clams open and potatoes are tender. Remove from heat and season with salt and pepper to taste.

To serve, divide the opened clams among soup bowls, and ladle the chowder over them.

WINE SUGGESTION:
Pinot Gris has a tendency toward textural richness, which is perfect for this rich clam chowder. Chill a glass of Pinot Gris from Oregon with its pretty pear and almond blossom flavors and feel the bliss.

The Scallop Festival, now in its forty-fourth year, originated with a group of local fishermen who wanted to celebrate their catch. Over the years it's been held in several different locations. Now, rain or shine, it's housed in a huge tent on Main Street in Bourne, near the train station on the scenic Cape Cod Canal and Railroad Bridge (the second-largest lift bridge in the United States).

Held in September (the third weekend after Labor Day, Friday through Sunday), the festival is one of the biggest events on Cape Cod. Each year over fifty thousand people show up to feast on sea scallops,

herb-roasted chicken, and fish and chips. There is also a large food court with a variety of other foods and wine and beer. The festival includes an arts and craft show, a huge midway of rides and games for the kids, and live entertainment by local musicians in the main tent. It is a family-oriented event put on by the Cape Cod Canal Region Chamber of Commerce.

Marie Oliva, president and CEO of the chamber, says, "This isn't your average festival. The community has a big stake in the event, helping to make sure the Fest is superbly organized and enjoyable. Over 600 volunteers

PHOTOS BY DEB JOHNSON

help man the Fest to accommodate over 50,000 people who come to Cape Cod from all over the country. Buses and trains bring groups of people as well. It's the type of event that truly brings everyone together for a great time." In fact the Scallop Festival has been cited by the American Bus Association as one of "The Top 100 Events in North America" three times.

Because of the huge crowds, many people take the Cape Cod Central Railroad, which offers "Ride the Rails" travel packages from Hyannis to Buzzards Bay.

Cape Cod is known for sea scallops and bay scallops. The scallops are used for the festival and available year-round. They come from the deeper waters around the Cape. Cape or bay scallops are seasonal (October to April) and are harvested in the bays and inlets around the Cape.

For more information visit bournescallopfest.com or call (508) 759-6000, ext.10.

Original Scallop Fest Dinner Recipe

Compliments of Joe Agrillo, Chief Cook

The Scallop Festival is an enormous event. To give you an idea of its scope, here is the recipe for the famous Scallop Dinner Recipe that feeds the crowds.

1,200 pounds flour
1,200 pounds clam fry mix
96 pounds nondairy creamer
18 gallons eggs, broken and ready
60 gallons water, warm
60 gallons water, cold
4,000 pounds vegetable shortening
6,000 pounds scallops
6,000 pounds french fries
3,500 pounds coleslaw

Special equipment: friolater

Thoroughly mix flour and clam fry mix in large shallow pan. Set aside.

Mix nondairy creamer and eggs with warm water and whip together until mixed thoroughly. Let stand 15 minutes at room temperature. Add cold water and whip thoroughly.

Heat shortening in friolater to 360°F frying temperature.

Place 2 cups scallops into a 10-inch-round wire mesh basket and dredge into flour and clam fry mix coating scallops well with the mixture. Shake well to remove excess flour.

Put coated scallops into egg wash mixture.

Place dipped scallops into first basket and dredge in flour and clam fry mix mixture a second time.

Place dredged scallops into fryer basket and cook in friolater until golden brown.

Place on paper towels to drain.

Continue this procedure repeatedly until all are cooked!

Serve with french fries and coleslaw.

CROW FARM

192 ROUTE 6A
EAST SANDWICH, MA 02563
(508) 888-0690
OWNERS: PAUL CROWELL AND FAMILY

After a long winter, Crow Farm is one of those special places one looks forward to opening in May. At the beginning of the month, you'll find jams, jellies, and local honey. But by the end of the month, when it's time to plant on Cape Cod, you'll find enough for your own instant garden. Choose from tomatoes, peas, cucumbers, eggplant, a variety of peppers (regular and hot), squashes, and herbs that were started months ago in Crow Farm's greenhouses. As the summer season builds, so does the bounty in this small white building, nestled by the side of the road in East Sandwich. It starts with different lettuces and fresh flowers in June and continues into July with juicy yellow and white peaches and corn. Crow Farm is one of the few farms on the Cape that still grows and sells local corn. In late summer there are crisp varieties of apples. When fall hits, it's time to fill the gardens and pathways with abundantly colored mums and pumpkins. And toward Christmas you can pick up your tree, a wreath, or a lovely poinsettia plant.

In addition to this bounty of fruits, vegetables, and flowers there's Ellen Crowell's baked goods. Homemade breads and pies made with homegrown fruits are popular with locals and tourists. And the fact that all this happens on a farm that has been owned by the same family for almost one hundred years seems to add to the flavor. Crow Farm began in 1916 when brothers David and Lincoln Crowell purchased forty acres of land. Paul Crowell is the third generation to work the farm, and his son Jason will be the fourth. Stop by to experience this Cap Cod treasure.

ELLEN CROWELL'S BLUEBERRY BREAD

(SERVES 6–8)

1 cup plus 2 tablespoons sugar, divided
½ cup (4 ounces) unsalted butter, slightly softened
2 eggs
1½ teaspoons vanilla extract
2 cups all-purpose flour
2 teaspoons baking powder
½ teaspoon salt
½ cup milk
2½ cups fresh blueberries, washed, dried, and
   picked over

Preheat oven to 375°F.

Butter an 8½ X 4–inch loaf pan and set aside. Combine 1 cup sugar and the butter in a large mixing bowl and beat with an electric mixer until light and fluffy. Add the eggs, one at a time, beating well after each addition. Add the vanilla and mix well.

Combine the flour, baking powder, and salt in another bowl. Add the dry ingredients to the batter in three additions, alternating with the milk.

Gently fold in the blueberries and pour the batter into the prepared pan. Sprinkle the remaining 2 tablespoons sugar over the batter and bake until a toothpick inserted in the center comes out clean, 50 to 60 minutes. Cool in a pan for 10 minutes and turn out on a rack to cool completely. Wrap and store at room temperature or refrigerate

Dunbar Tea Shop

1 Water Street
Sandwich, MA 02563
(508) 833-2485
DUNBARTEASHOP.COM
Chef/Owner: Paula Hegarty

The Dunbar Tea Shop is located in Sandwich, one of the oldest and most picturesque towns on Cape Cod, and it keeps company with some of the most historic buildings in town. Next door is the First Church of Christ, built in 1830 and with a spire designed by noted English architect Christopher Wren. Across the street is the Dexter Grist Mill, built in 1640, and up the street is one of the oldest houses on the Cape, the Hoxie House, also built in the 1600s. Sandwich became the center of American glassmaking in the early 1800s and is now home to the Sandwich Glass Museum.

I sat in the main room of the one of the best New England tearooms with chef and owner Paula Hegarty, who filled me in on the history of the Tea Room and the house,

which dates back to 1740. "My husband, Jim, and I bought it from a couple from England who fell in love with the house and area. It reminded them of England. When they arrived they did not know this room (the main part of the tea room with the original fireplace) was here. The building was totally overgrown with vegetation. They found this room and decided it would make a nice tearoom. It was cleaned up, and they used a hot plate for their kitchen. Later, they turned the main house into a B&B and lived in part of the house." The shop takes its name from Colonel and Mrs. Henry Dunbar, who bought the house in the 1920s. While Colonel Dunbar worked on the Cape Cod Canal, Mrs. Dunbar gave tea parties. The Hegartys are only the fifth owners of the property.

There are two businesses under the roof—the Dunbar Tea Room and the Dunbar Tea Shop. Paula is very much attached to the retail part of the business. "We have a large selection of loose teas and a variety of teapots and cups from elegant to whimsical. Then I decided to get involved with the cooking. I am a pretty good cook, I like to cook, and I can do it!" Bumbleberry Pie is one of Paula's signature dishes.

BUMBLEBERRY PIE

(SERVES 6–8)

For the filling:

1½ cups blueberries, washed and picked over
1½ cups strawberries, washed, stemmed, and cut in half
1½ cups blackberries
1½ cups raspberries
1½ cups all-purpose flour
1½ cups sugar
1 teaspoon ground cinnamon
½ teaspoon ground nutmeg
½ teaspoon ground ginger

For the topping:

¾ cup all-purpose flour
¾ cup sugar
6 tablespoons unsalted butter, slightly softened
Grated zest of 1 orange

To assemble the dish:

1 (10-inch) unbaked pie shell

For the filling: Preheat oven to 350°F. Combine the berries in a large bowl. In another bowl, combine the flour, sugar, and spices and mix well. Add to the berries and toss gently until evenly mixed.

For the topping: Place the flour, sugar, butter, and orange zest in a bowl and mix with a fork or with your fingers, working in the butter just until large moist clumps form.

To assemble the dish: Gently turn the berries into the pie shell and distribute the topping over the filling. Bake until the juices bubble, about 1 hour and 10 minutes.

Dunbar Scone Recipe

(MAKES 15 SCONES)

For the scones:

6 cups all-purpose flour

¼ cup sugar

1½ tablespoons baking powder

½ teaspoon kosher salt

1 cup cold unsalted butter, cut into about 12 pieces

1 cup dried cranberries, optional

1½ cups half-and-half

Egg wash (1 egg beaten with 1 teaspoon water)

For the optional glaze:

1 cup confectioner's sugar

2 teaspoons milk

¼ teaspoon orange extract

For the scones: Preheat oven to 400°F. Combine flour, sugar, baking powder, and salt in a food processor bowl fitted with a steel blade; pulse a few times to blend. Add butter; pulse to small pea-size pieces.

Turn mixture into a large bowl and add the dried cranberries, if using. Make a well in the center of the flour mixture and add the half-and-half, tossing with a fork or clean hands until moistened completely; bring mixture together to form a ball.

Turn dough out onto a floured surface and sprinkle with a little flour. Roll or pat dough out gently to about 1-inch thickness. Cut out scones using a 2½-inch round biscuit cutter dipped in flour. Gently reroll scraps to form a few more scones and transfer them to a parchment-lined baking sheet, spaced about 2 inches apart. Brush tops of scones lightly with egg wash and bake until golden, about 18 minutes. Transfer to a rack to cool. Serve slightly warm or at room temperature.

For the optional glaze: Combine confectioner's sugar, milk, and orange extract in a small bowl, mixing until thoroughly blended and smooth. Drizzle over completely cooled scones.

The Glass Onion

37 North Main Street
Falmouth, MA 02540
(508) 540-3730
THEGLASSONIONDINING.COM
Owners: Josh and Tally Christian
Chef: Tim Miller

The Glass Onion is located in the heart of Falmouth's Historic Queens Byway on Route 28 as you head into Falmouth Center. This elegant but casual restaurant is owned and operated by Josh and Tally Christian. I met Josh several years ago when he was a waiter at a restaurant in the mid-Cape area. At that time he had wishes and dreams about having his own place. Today his dreams have come true, and he has created one of the most consistent, high-end, stylish restaurants on the Cape, in the town where he was born.

Josh manages and runs the front of the house, while Tally is the behind-the-scenes manager, except on Friday and Saturday nights when she is in the front of the house

with Josh. The three-year-old restaurant has received major raves for its inventive and delicious menu, professional service, comfortable atmosphere, and beautiful decor. Above the old, white Cape Cod wainscoting, the walls are painted lovely sea foam green. It is the perfect setting for a romantic dinner or special occasion. The Glass Onion is open for dinner only.

Chef Tim Miller presides over the kitchen with his innovative dishes. The Lobster Strudel, made with mascarpone, has become one of the restaurant's signature dishes. Another favorite is Oysters on the Half Shell, served with a cucumber mignonette sauce, lemon, and extra-virgin olive oil. The oysters are provided by a local oyster farmer, Les Hemmila of Barnstable Seafarms. Tally's mother, Sally Talmadge, is the bread maker for the restaurant, making thirty-five to forty loaves a day. And for dessert the Lavender Chèvre Cheesecake with Blueberry Compote should not be missed.

LOBSTER STRUDEL

(SERVES 8)

For the lobster filling:

8 ounces fresh lobster meat, diced

½ cup mascarpone cheese

Juice and zest of ½ large lemon

½ teaspoon chopped fresh tarragon

½ teaspoon chopped fresh parsley

½ teaspoon chopped fresh chives

Salt and pepper to taste

For the strudel:

1 (16-ounce) box phyllo dough, thawed

½ cup unsalted butter, melted

For the sauce:

½ cup lobster stock (page 136)

2 tablespoons heavy cream

½ cup unsalted butter, cut in cubes and softened

Fresh lemon juice to taste

Salt and pepper to taste

For the lobster filling: Combine the lobster, cheese, lemon juice and zest, and herbs in a bowl. Toss gently until evenly mixed; season with salt and pepper to taste. Cover and refrigerate until needed.

For the strudel: Preheat oven to 475°F. Stack 2 sheets of phyllo on a large clean, dry work surface. With a pastry brush, very lightly coat the entire surface of the dough with melted butter.

Using a sharp knife, cut the dough in half crosswise to make two 9 x 14 rectangles. Place ⅛ of the lobster filling along the bottom (short side) of each rectangle, leaving about a ½-inch border all around. Fold the bottom border of dough up and over the length of the lobster filling, then fold in the sides. Carefully and evenly roll up the dough jelly roll style to completely enclose the filling. Repeat the process three more times to make 8 strudels in all.

Arrange strudels seam side down on a parchment-lined baking sheet so they are not touching and brush with melted butter. Bake until golden brown, about 6 to 8 minutes.

For the sauce: Combine stock and cream in saucepan over medium heat and bring to a simmer. Cook until thickened and reduced to about 3 tablespoons. Remove from heat and whisk in butter, a little at a time, until incorporated. Season to taste with lemon juice and salt and pepper.

To assemble the dish: Place one strudel on each serving plate and spoon sauce over it. Serve immediately.

Lavender Chèvre Cheesecake with Blueberry Compote
(SERVES 12)

For the cheesecake:

12 ounces chèvre (goat cheese), room temperature

10 ounces cream cheese, room temperature

½ cup sugar

½ cup honey

¼ cup all-purpose flour

Zest and juice of 1 large orange (about 2 teaspoons zest and 3 tablespoons juice)

1 teaspoon finely chopped dried lavender buds

1 teaspoon kosher salt

8 eggs, separated, room temperature

1¼ cup mascarpone cheese

4 tablespoons sugar

For the compote (yields about 1 1/2 cups):

2 cups fresh blueberries

3 tablespoons water

¼ cup granular sugar

2 tablespoons lemon juice

½ teaspoon lemon zest

To make the cheesecake: Preheat oven to 350°F. Generously butter 12 (8-ounce) ramekins and place side by side in a roasting pan just large enough to hold them all. Set aside. Bring a large pot of water to boil.

Combine the chèvre and cream cheese in the bowl of an electric mixer fitted with a paddle attachment. Beat on medium speed just until creamy and smooth, scraping down the sides of the bowl several times (do not overmix). Add the sugar, honey, flour, orange zest, lavender, and salt; mix just until thoroughly blended. With the mixer on low speed, add the egg yolks one at a time, beating just to incorporate before adding the next. Add the mascarpone and orange juice and continue beating just until thoroughly blended. Set batter aside.

Replace the mixer's paddle attachment with the whisk attachment and place the egg whites in a clean mixer bowl. Beat on medium speed until thick and foamy. Add the sugar, 1 tablespoon at a time, and continue beating until soft peaks form. Fold a third of the whites into the batter to lighten, then add the rest of the egg whites, folding quickly and carefully until no streaks remain.

Divide the batter among the prepared ramekins and place the roasting pan in the oven. Carefully add just enough boiling water to the roasting pan to come halfway up the outsides of the ramekins. Lay a sheet of aluminum foil lightly over the ramekins and bake until they just jiggle in the center, about 30 minutes. One at a time, carefully remove ramekins from the water bath and transfer to a wire rack to cool.

To make the compote: Put 1½ cups of blueberries, water, and sugar, in a medium saucepan, reserving ½ cup of the blueberries. Bring to a boil; reduce heat to medium and cook for 10 minutes.

Add remaining blueberries, lemon juice, and zest and cook for another 6 to 8 minutes.

Spoon the compote, 1 or 2 tablespoons, over each dessert before serving.

WINE SUGGESTION:
Brut Reserve Champagne. Bright citrus fruit, crushed flowers and mineral notes, along with plenty of length and focus in the finish, and a naturally lilting acidity make it an excellent choice for rich lobster. It's also a wonderful vehicle to lift the savoriness of the goat cheese cake to new heights.

HOW DO YOU LIKE YOUR OYSTERS?

There are as many toppings for oysters on the half shell as there are oysters. I asked a few chefs for their favorites.

TIM MILLER
Chef at The Glass Onion (page 44)

On each oyster, drizzle ⅛ teaspoon lemon juice, ¼ teaspoon good-quality extra-virgin olive oil, and a pinch fresh minced chives; then serve.

REBECCA ARNOLD
Former Chef at Pain D'Avignon (page 106)

Mignonette Sauce

¼ cup champagne or chardonnay vinegar
1 teaspoon freshly crushed black pepper
½ teaspoon sugar
2 tablespoons water

Whisk all the ingredients together. "The sauce should be slightly sweet, slightly sour, and quite peppery." Top oysters with sauce.

FLORENCE LOWELL
Executive Chef/Owner at the Naked Oyster (page 100)

Cucumber Sake and Ginger Mignonette

½ cucumber with skin, finely diced
1 teaspoon freshly grated ginger root
Salt and black pepper to taste
1 cup premium sake

Add ingredients to sake. Chill for 2 hours before topping chilled oysters with a teaspoon of sauce.

Do It Yourself Cocktail Sauce

This is one of the most popular sauces for oysters. Cocktail sauce is just freshly grated (or jarred) horseradish added to ketchup to taste. Or sometimes it is just a squeeze of lemon, depending on your taste.

MAC HAY
Owner/Chef of Mac's Shack (page 53)

Top each oyster with finely minced chorizo and a dash nuoc mam (Vietnamese fish sauce). Place under the broiler just until the edges of the oysters start to curl (2 minutes or less). Serve immediately.

MARTHA KANE
Chef/Owner at FIN (page 84)

For each oyster squeeze a few drops fresh lemon juice topped with a touch of freshly grated horseradish to taste.

MICHAEL CERALDI
Chef at Dalla Cucina (page 140)

This is Chef Ceraldi's special topping served for New Year's Eve.

Prosecco Granita
1 bottle Prosecco
2 whole shallots, peeled
2 fresh bay leaves
¼ cup granulated sugar
½ teaspoon salt
Pomegranate seeds

Combine all ingredients in a saucepan over medium-low heat and reduce by half. Remove the bay leaves and shallots. Pour liquid into shallow plastic storage container and place in the freezer for 4 to 6 hours, until frozen solid. Using a metal spoon, scrape the top of the frozen ice, pulling the spoon toward you, to create the granita. The scraped granita can be stored in the freezer in another plastic storage container, or it can be scraped as needed.
Top each chilled oyster with the granita and several pomegranate seeds and serve.

SHUCKING OYSTERS

You will need a real oyster knife found in any hardware or fish market on the Cape. Gloves are advised, at least one on the hand that is holding the oyster, but a towel will work just as well. I have found it's best to put the oysters in the freezer for about 15 minutes before shucking.

If using a small towel, drape it in your hand over the oyster, flat side up, or place it on a firm surface. Make sure to hold the oyster firmly. Slip the point of the knife between the top and bottom shells between the hinge.

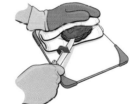

Using a twisting motion, pry the two shells apart, making sure not to lose any of the liquid inside.

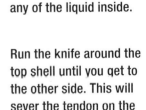

Run the knife around the top shell until you get to the other side. This will sever the tendon on the top of the shell.

Slide the knife under the oyster to cut it free from its shell (it will be connected by a tough knob). Place the oyster on a bed of crushed ice and serve with your favorite topping.

ILLUSTRATIONS BY
ROBERT PRINCE

FRIED OYSTERS
FRIED CLAMS
CLAM CHOWDER
FRIED CALAMARI
EAT THIS SHELLFISH

The Wellfleet OysterFest is a two-day (Saturday and Sunday) event held the weekend after Columbus Day in October in a variety of locations in the town of Wellfleet. It is produced by Shellfish Promotion and Tasting (SPAT), a nonprofit organization devoted to fostering a greater understanding of the history and traditions of the town's shellfishing Industry. The acronym honors the oyster, which begins life as a free-swimming larva called spat. SPAT is also committed to educating the public about preserving traditional shellfishing practices and the creation of new shellfishing technologies.

The OysterFest began in 2001 and now includes seminars, a shucking contest, a 5K road race, an arts and crafts fair, and cooking demonstrations. You can also choose to spend the entire weekend in and around Town Hall, sampling the wide variety of foods supplied by Cape

restaurants and food vendors. Hot foods, cold foods, and raw foods are all there. There's also fine dining, informal dining, and music. The schedule of events is posted at the website, and a visit there is essential.

Mac Hay is the owner of Mac's Shack in Wellfleet and president of SPAT's board of directors. He says, "The OysterFest provides and enhances a way of bringing the Wellfleet community together as well as preserving an important way of life here. It also brings people in. This is great exposure for the Lower Cape on what otherwise would be a down, off-season weekend. Most activities and restaurants end and close after Columbus Day. This event extends the season a little. It's the big fall finale before we go into the winter months here on the Cape."

For more information visit wellfleetoysterfest.org.

Green Briar Jam Kitchen

Thornton W. Burgess Society
6 Discovery Hill Road
East Sandwich, MA 02567
(508) 888-6870
THORNTONBURGESS.ORG

The Jam Kitchen dates back to 1903, when Ida Putman, the original owner, inherited her mother's house in East Sandwich. Ida decided to open a tearoom and served tea, toast, sandwiches, and cake. It was not a success. Ida didn't have much experience in the kitchen and in truth was not a good cook. However, her preserves were a hit, so Ida got herself a copy of *Fannie Farmer* and taught herself the art of preserving fruit.

Ida's perseverance for making jams and jellies paid off. The business continued to grow. Martha Blake started working in the kitchen when she was seventeen and purchased the business from Ida Putman thirty years later. In 1977 Martha celebrated her seventy-fifth birthday and wanted to retire. She was single-handedly putting up eleven thousand jars of preserves a season and ready to sell. But unfortunately there were no takers. In 1979 the Thornton W. Burgess Society, a fledging environmental education organization based in Sandwich, bought it. The society didn't plan to keep it as a jam kitchen, but Martha donated Ida's original recipes in the event that someday they might be put to use. Then in 1980 the Society decided to reopen the Jam Kitchen, and the building was back in full operation. Martha came back and volunteered her services until she was into her nineties. She died on July 6, 2002.

Mizue Murphy worked under Martha Blake in the kitchen and is still there today guarding most of the recipe secrets. She is pictured here preparing a recipe for Bread and Butter Pickles.

Visiting the Green Briar Jam Kitchen is a major treat in many ways. Take a tour and you'll be able to experience the fragrant aromas of fruits and preserves coming from the kettles used by Ida and Martha as they simmer on the old black burners. Observe the sun-cooked fruits under the glass structure in the gift shop. This is a place where time stands still and a tradition is kept alive.

SUN-COOKED PEACHES

(MAKES 6 PINTS)

4 pounds peaches
4 pounds sugar (about 9 cups)
1 cup brandy

To skin the peaches, cut an X through just the skin on the bottom of each one. Put peaches in boiling water just until skins loosen a bit, 20 to 60 seconds. (Riper peaches require less time.) Transfer peaches to a bowl of ice water. One at a time, lift peaches out of the water bath and slip off the skins. Remove pits and slice fruit to ½-inch thickness.

Combine peaches and sugar in a shallow enamel or a glass pan. Cover with a clear glass lid or plastic wrap and place in full sun for several days in a protected area. At the end of the cooking process, pour brandy over the fruit. Pour into 8-ounce sterilized jars and process to seal.

BREAD & BUTTER PICKLES

(MAKES ABOUT 2 PINTS)

2 English or 5 pickling-size cucumbers
6 small white (boiling) onions peeled and thinly sliced
2 tablespoons coarse pickling salt
3 cups white grape juice simmered and reduced by half
⅔ cup cider vinegar
⅓ teaspoon whole mustard seed
¼ teaspoon celery seed
½ teaspoon black pepper
¼ teaspoon turmeric powder
1 cup sugar

Scour the cucumbers lengthwise with the tines of fork. Slice crosswise ⅜-inch thick.

Put cucumbers, onions, and pickling salt in a bowl and toss to coat. Let stand for 30 minutes then rinse in cold water. Transfer to a large non-aluminum pot then add the grape juice, vinegar, spices, and sugar. Bring to a boil over high heat, stirring to dissolve the sugar. Boil 5 minutes and remove from heat. Pour into two sterilized pint jars and seal.

Quicks Hole

6 Luscombe Avenue
Woods Hole, MA 02543
(508) 495-0792
quicksholewickedfresh.com
Owner: Beth Colt
Chef: Stephanie Mikolazyk

This seasonal farm-to-table restaurant is on the ground floor of the Woods Hole Inn and sits on a corner facing the Woods Hole Ferry. The building, built in 1898, was for sale and in dire need of repair. Beth Colt, formerly in the entertainment business in Los Angeles, bought the building and opened the restaurant and inn. Here you'll find the commitment to using local ingredients illustrated in their salads and seafood, especially the Sippewissett, Cuttyhunk, and Washburn Island oysters.

Chef Stephanie Mikolazyk comes from a family of commercial fishermen in a small port town in Rhode Island. Several years spent living on the West Coast have given her a very Californian take on New England traditions and created quite a buzz around this unique restaurant. "The menu is 100 percent mine. My lobster tacos are one of the specialties of the house, but I make other seafood, pork and chicken burritos, quesadillas, and salads." For drinks, try the special cold sangria or a chilled local beer.

If you are there in the early evening you can eat, drink, and watch the spectacular sunset over the harbor. And if you are a cycling enthusiast, take the eight-mile Shining Sea Bikeway from Bourne to Woods Hole. You'll pass sandy beaches, salt marshes, and shoreside ponds before emerging at Little Harbor in Woods Hole. Have lunch at Quicks Hole and then hop back on the trail.

LOCAL!!
FRESH!!

★ MORNING GLORY FARM - MARTHA'S VINEYARD

★ ATLANTIC OYSTER - WAQUOIT

★ CLAM MAN - FALMOUTH

★ ALLEN FARMS - WESTPORT

★ COONAMESSET FARMS - FALMOUTH

★ NOBSKA FARM - WOODS HOLE

LOBSTER TACOS

(SERVES 6)

For the lobster:

3 pounds fresh lobster meat, cut into bite-size pieces
1 cup mayonnaise
½ cup chopped fresh basil or tarragon
¼ cup fresh lemon or lime juice (from 1 lemon or 2 limes)
Salt and pepper to taste

For the pico de gallo:

6 Roma tomatoes, seeded and diced
1 cup diced red onion
1 cup chopped fresh cilantro
½ cup fresh lime juice (from 2 limes)
3 garlic cloves, finely chopped
Salt and pepper to taste

For the Baja sauce:

1 cup sour cream
1 cup chopped fresh cilantro
½ cup mayonnaise
½ cup fresh lime juice (from 2 limes)
3 poblano peppers, charred, peeled, stemmed, seeded, and chopped
2 tablespoons hot sauce

To assemble the dish:

12 (6-inch) corn or flour tortillas
½ small head green cabbage, cored and shredded
Queso fresco (Mexican farmer's cheese), or regular farmer's cheese

For the lobster: Combine the lobster meat, mayonnaise, basil, and lemon or lime juice in a bowl and toss gently until evenly mixed. Add salt and pepper to taste. Set aside.

For the pico de gallo: Combine the ingredients in a bowl and mix well. Season with salt and pepper and set aside.

For the Baja sauce: Place the ingredients in a food processor fitted with a steel blade and blend until smooth. Transfer mixture to a squeeze bottle.

To assemble the dish: Place 2 tortillas on each plate. Mound some cabbage on each tortilla. Divide the lobster meat among the tortillas and top each with 2 to 3 tablespoons pico de gallo, a sprinkle of *queso fresco,* and a drizzle of Baja sauce.

Most of the food at Quicks Hole is served with their famous Sangria.

SAGAMORE INN

1131 ROUTE 6A
SAGAMORE, MA 02561
(508) 888-9707
SAGAMOREINNCAPECOD.COM
OWNERS: SUZANNE AND MICHAEL BILADEAU
CHEF: NORMAN MARCEAN

The Sagamore Inn dates back to the 1930s. While it has not functioned as an inn since the early part of the last century, it still retains the charm of its past. The dining room, which seats about 125, has its original tin ceiling, and some of the walls are tongue-in-groove paneling. A NO DANCING sign from World War II is still tacked on the wall next to the bar. The beautiful wood floors are sanded and polished each spring. For many years the inn was run as a pizza business by owners Fiorello (Bill) and Severona Bianco, who were from the Piedmont region of Italy. Eventually they wanted to retire, but they also wanted to keep the business going, so the inn was rented to Shirley and Joseph (Paddy) Pagliarani, both natives of Cape Cod. In an interview Shirley, now eighty-three, sat in my kitchen and told me stories about the early days at the inn.

"At that time Paddy did not have ten cents in his pocket, so we kept the pizza business going. I started to work on other main dishes for the restaurant menu, mostly Italian dishes and seafood. I even dug quahogs (clams) for my chowder. I was at the restaurant at five thirty every morning making all the sauces, soups, chowders, and my signature dish—forty-five pounds of pot roast with my 'bodacious' gravy. Paddy

managed and cooked in the kitchen. This was not just a two-person operation—it was a family affair; we had forty-three local people working for us, and many of our children would also pitch in."

Shirley and Paddy ran the inn for forty-five years. It was sold just before Paddy passed away to Suzanne and Michael Biladeau. The Biladeaus still have the same chef, former CIA man Norman Marcean, who's been cooking at the Inn for thirty-four years. Suzanne, Michael, and Norman maintain the original feel of the inn, with seafood platters, Italian pasta dishes, eggplant Parmesan, and Shirley's Yankee Pot Roast, which still appears on the menu along with the traditional bread and grape nut custard puddings.

Sagamore Inn's Grape Nut Custard Pudding

(SERVES 8–10)

1 cup Post Grape Nuts Cereal
4 cups warm milk
4 large eggs, beaten
¾ cup granulated sugar
¼ teaspoon salt
1 teaspoon pure vanilla extract
½ teaspoon ground cinnamon or
    ¼ teaspoon nutmeg (or both)

Preheat oven to 350°F.

Put the cereal in a medium-size bowl and pour the milk over it. Let stand 5 minutes.

In another medium-size bowl, add the eggs, sugar, salt, vanilla, and cinnamon and/or nutmeg. Whisk until well combined.

Add the milk and cereal to the egg mixture and stir well. Pour into a buttered 9 x 13 x 2-inch baking dish set inside a larger pan filled with hot water (called a bain-marie or water bath). Bake about 45 to 60 minutes or until a knife inserted in center comes out clean.

SHIRLEY'S YANKEE POT ROAST

(SERVES 6)

For the roast:

4–5 pound beef boneless chuck roast
(For best results, look for a piece that is
well marbled with fat.)
Salt and pepper to taste
2 tablespoons olive oil or rendered beef fat
1½ cups coarsely chopped onions
1½ cups coarsely chopped carrots
1½ cups coarsely chopped celery
½ cup water

For the gravy:

¾ cup cold water
3 tablespoons all-purpose flour

For the roast: Season the roast generously with salt and pepper. Heat the oil in an 8-quart deep-sided cast iron pot or Dutch oven over high heat and carefully add the meat to the pan. Sear well on all sides; transfer to a plate.

Add onions to the pan drippings and cook, stirring, until golden and translucent, about 5 minutes. Return meat to the pan along with the carrots, celery, water, and salt and pepper to taste. Bring to a boil, cover the pot, and adjust the heat to a simmer. Cook, turning occasionally, until meat is tender, about 4 hours. Remove from heat. Remove the meat and vegetables from the braising liquid and discard the vegetables.

For the gravy: Return the pot to high heat and bring the braising liquid to a boil. Place the water in a small bowl and gradually add the flour, whisking constantly to form a smooth slurry. Add the slurry to the boiling liquid gradually, whisking constantly until mixture thickens to gravy consistency.

Return the meat to the pan to heat through. Slice the roast and serve with the gravy over mashed potatoes. This is what Shirley calls her "Bodacious Gravy."

WINE SUGGESTION:
Cabernet Sauvignon. This old-fashioned pot roast recipe deserves a classic American red wine which is full-bodied, complex and elegant with ample tannins. Look for a Cabernet Sauvignon from Napa Valley or Washington state.

The Seafood Shanty

803 Scenic Highway, Route 6
Bournedale, MA 02532
(508) 888-0040
THESEAFOODSHANTY.NET
Owners/Chef: Tish and Johnny
Economides

A good place to begin your Cape Cod adventure is the Seafood Shanty in Bournedale, along the Cape Cod Canal. Located almost at the midpoint between the Sagamore and Bourne Bridges, the Seafood Shanty is one of the Cape's best-kept secrets. You'll find a delicious lobster roll filled with tender chunks of lobster and just enough mayonnaise. It's what a lobster roll should be, simple and traditional. It is served on a toasted hot dog roll with a side of coleslaw or french fries.

Tish (short for Patricia) and Johnny Economides have run this seasonal business for over twenty-two years. Family-run until the kids struck out on their own, today Tish and Johnny operate the Shanty with a group of students. Johnny has worked in restaurants all his life and does the cooking. "My parents owned a business in Falmouth called Joan and Ted's in the 1960s." Take a look in the back of the Shanty and you can see the sign. "I make and serve the food the way we like it. That goes for the portion size and the way it is presented. Everything is homemade and made to order. All our fish and shellfish are fresh and bought from local vendors."

Order your food, sit in one of the Adirondack chairs, and take in the view of the boats passing by on the Canal. The portions are generous, and the service is fast and efficient. They don't serve alcohol, but you're welcome to bring your own beer or wine. You won't find a more perfect setting!

Lobster Roll

(SERVES 1)

8 ounces freshly cooked lobster meat, cut in
   bite-size pieces

½–1 teaspoon mayonnaise

Salt and pepper to taste

1 large leaf romaine or Boston lettuce

1 hot dog roll, buttered and toasted golden

Place the lobster meat in a bowl and add the mayonnaise and salt and pepper, tossing to coat. Tuck the lettuce leaf lengthwise into the bottom of the roll, pile the lobster meat over the lettuce, and serve with a cold beer from Cape Cod Beer Company (page 72).

MID CAPE

BRAZILIAN GRILL

680 MAIN STREET
HYANNIS, MA 02601
(508) 771-0109
BRAZILIANGRILL-CAPECOD.COM
CHEF/OWNER: MASSIMILIANO DE PAULO

It's called the Brazilian Grill and serves Churrascaria, which means "Rotisserie Barbeque." This wonderfully unique restaurant is located in the west end of Hyannis, and you will not find a dining experience like it anywhere else on Cape Cod.

The creative force behind this twelve-year-old restaurant is Massimiliano De Paulo. "I have been in this country for eighteen years and started working in restaurants washing dishes, then as a chef," he says. "I have been saving my money since I arrived here. A large Brazilian community exists on Cape Cod, and I found the opportunity to open this restaurant."

When you enter the restaurant, you immediately feel the warmth and helpfulness of the staff. Ranato, the headwaiter, suggests a Caipirinha, the national cocktail of Brazil, to start. He then explains the ordering system: On each table are small round tokens. "It works like a traffic light. On one side are red and the other green. When you are ready for your meat course, turn your token to the green side and one of the servers, or Gauchos, will come to your table with a knife and skewer, on which are speared various kinds of meat. We have ten to fifteen cuts of meat; beef, pork, chicken, and lamb are the most popular. The meat is cut, the pieces roll off the knife, and you pick up the small tongs next to your plate and bring the meat to your plate. When finished, turn the token to the red side." This is important to remember, because the Brazilian Grill offers a fixed-price, all-you-can-eat menu. At the rear of the restaurant you'll find a buffet with a variety of salads, vegetables, grains, sliced meats, soups, and even sushi. The Butternut Squash Soup is a favorite of Chef De Paulo's. There's also a number of traditional Brazilian favorites, such as rice and beans, sausages, and fried bananas. And, of course, a large selection of desserts. Everything is made fresh and in-house. Bring your appetite and enjoy a bit of Brazil on Cape Cod.

CAIPIRINHA

(SERVES 1)

1 or 2 limes, quartered
2 teaspoons superfine sugar
2 ounces cachaca

Place the lime wedges and sugar into an Old Fashioned glass and crush the lime into the sugar.

Fill the glass with ice cubes.

Pour in the cachaca and stir well.

Cape Cod Beer Company, Inc.

1336 Phinney's Lane
Hyannis, MA 02601
(508) 790-4200
CAPECODBEER.COM
Owners: Beth and Todd Marcus

In 1998 Beth and Todd Marcus moved from Philadelphia to Cape Cod to be closer to their families. Todd has a degree in electrical engineering, but his real passion has been in the breweries; at one time it was his hobby. His new career started when he answered an ad for a brewmaster at Hyannisport Brewing Company (HBC) in Hyannis. At the time it was the only local brewery in the area. It was a microbrewery with a restaurant attached to it. Todd got the job and worked there for five years, until the brewer closed its doors.

Beth and Todd decided to buy the equipment and start their own business here on the Cape. They are now in their ninth year.

"We are all about local and think of ourselves as champions of all things local!" Beth explains. They keep the distribution within a fifty-mile radius of the brewery to make sure the product is kept fresh. "We are passionate about our product, to say the least. It's like our first child," she goes on to say.

For Beth and Todd it is all about customer service, quality, community, and conservation. But some say, "It's all about the marketing," and while they don't disagree, it's really about their passion for their beer!

The Marcuses open the brewery to the public for guided tours. Check their website for hours of operation. And while you are there, take home a gallon of their delicious beer.

Spent Grain Cheese Crackers

(MAKES ABOUT 8 DOZEN CRACKERS)

2 cups (16 ounces) grated sharp cheddar cheese

½ cup (1 stick) unsalted butter, cut in pieces

1 cup all-purpose flour

¼ teaspoon salt

Cayenne pepper to taste

½ cup chopped pecans

½ cup spent grain

Combine the cheese and butter in a food processor fitted with a steel blade. Process until well blended. Add the flour, salt, and cayenne; pulse to blend. Add the pecans and spent grain and pulse several times to evenly incorporate. Do not overprocess the dough; it should be crumbly, not creamy, with visible bits of pecans.

Turn the dough out onto a sheet of parchment or waxed paper on a work surface. Shape the dough into a log about 1½ inches in diameter, wrap in plastic, and refrigerate for at least 1 hour.

Preheat oven to 350°F. Unwrap the chilled dough and place on a cutting board. With a sharp knife, slice the dough into ⅛-inch-thick rounds and arrange ¼ inch apart on a baking sheet lined with parchment paper. Bake the crackers until lightly browned, 10 to 12 minutes. Transfer to a rack to cool. Store crackers in an airtight container up to 2 weeks.

Spicy Beer Brittle

(FILLS 1 [12 X 17-INCH] SHEET PAN)

2 cups sugar

1 cup light corn syrup

1 cup flat, room temperature Cape Cod Red Ale, or another amber ale

2 cups shelled raw or roasted peanuts

¼ teaspoon salt, if using raw peanuts

⅛ teaspoon chipotle chili powder, optional

1 tablespoon butter

1 teaspoon baking soda

1 teaspoon vanilla

Coat a rimmed baking sheet with butter or nonstick cooking spray. Combine the sugar, corn syrup, and beer in a large saucepan. Attach a candy thermometer to the side of the pan and place the pan over medium heat. Stir

continuously until sugar is completely dissolved. When mixture comes to a boil, watch closely until thermometer registers 245°F (soft ball stage).

Add peanuts (plus salt if using raw nuts) and chipotle chili powder and continue to cook until thermometer registers 300°F. Remove from heat and quickly add the butter, baking soda, and vanilla, stirring until evenly blended. Return to stove and cook 1 to 2 minutes more.

Remove from heat and immediately scrape the hot brittle onto the prepared baking sheet, spreading with a wooden spoon. Cool completely, then break into pieces. Store in an airtight container at room temperature up to 1 month.

Cape Cod Central Dinner Train

252 Main Street
Hyannis, MA 02601
(508) 771-3800
capetrain.com
Executive Chef: Richard Davis

While writing this book I talked to chefs about food, their cooking, and their experiences. But it was Chef Richard Davis who had the most unusual chef's job. He cooks on a moving train. He told me it is a very unique experience. "You have to go with the flow (in more than one respect) because of the motion of the train," he says. "It adds another element to cooking." According to Chef Davis everything is a matter of timing and, especially, balance. "My feet and legs have to be in the right position every minute while the train is moving. When I slice the tenderloin, my balance is extremely important because, if it isn't, I could slice off my hand."

Chef Davis has had his own business for twenty-eight years and has been a subcontractor for the railroad for seventeen years. He does all the food and beverages. The kitchen area in the train is extremely small. "You have the bar with drinks, the small dishwashing area, pots, pans, silverware, linens, and tableware. Orchestration in sequence and timing is critical," he explains. He also says that in the restaurant business it is important to have a good team. "You are only as good as your team. With a good team you win the game. Some of the people I work with have been here as long as I have. On Thanksgiving we did 220 dinners! It's kind of fun to work the train."

The train serves lunch and dinner. Board the lunch train in Hyannis at noon, or hop on the dinner train at six in the evening. The ride for dinner is about three hours. You can also have Sunday brunch on the train. That trip leaves Hyannis at eleven and comes back at one. The Central Dinner Train also offers a special Murder Mystery Dinner trip, a Taste of Italy trip, and a New Year's Gala. During the day the train goes along the Cape Cod Canal, where you can watch people biking on the service road and see boats in the canal. At night the lights of the passing towns flicker in the windows as you speed along the Cape. It's an experience not to be missed!

BREAST OF CHICKEN HOMMARDE

(SERVES 2)

For chicken:

¼ cup all-purpose flour
½ teaspoon salt
½ teaspoon freshly cracked black pepper
1 extra large egg, beaten well
½ teaspoon fresh chopped dill
3 tablespoons olive oil
2 chicken breasts

For Lobster Beurre Blanc:

1 stick butter
1 medium shallot, minced
¼ cup white wine
¼ cup heavy cream
Juice of 1 lemon
2 ounces fresh cooked lobster meat,
    cut into pieces

Preheat oven to 350°F.

For the chicken: Combine the flour, salt, and pepper in a shallow bowl. Combine the egg and dill in another shallow bowl; beat well to blend.

Heat the olive oil in a medium-size saucepan. Dredge the chicken breast in the flour, shaking off any excess; coat with the egg mixture letting the excess drip back in the bowl before carefully laying the chicken in the hot pan. Cook until brown on both sides 1 to 2 minutes per side. Transfer the chicken to a baking sheet and place in the oven to finish cooking, about 15 minutes.

For the Lobster Beurre Blanc: While the chicken is in the oven, return the sauté pan to medium heat and add 1 tablespoon of the butter. Add the shallot and sauté until translucent about 5 minutes. Add the wine and heavy cream and simmer until reduced and thickened. Remove pan from heat and gradually whisk in the remaining butter. Add the lobster meat and mix well.

To plate: Place the chicken breasts on two serving plates, top each with lobster meat, and divide the Beurre Blanc between the two portions.

WINE SUGGESTION:
Ribolla Gialla. An Italian Ribolla Gialla from Friuli is both rich and full-bodied with orchard fruit flavors and an undertone of spiciness, which has the stuffing to complement the wow factor of the chicken topped with lobster.

CENTERVILLE PIE COMPANY

1671 FALMOUTH ROAD
CENTERVILLE, MA 02632
(774) 470-1406
CENTERVILLEPIES.COM
OWNERS: LAURIE BOWMAN AND KRISTIN BROADLEY

Laurie Bowman's signature chicken pot pie had been very popular among family and friends. In fact it became so popular and the demand became so great that she and friend Kristin Broadley decided to make a business of it. In 2009 they realized a long-held dream when they opened their own restaurant and pie company. The Centerville Pie Company opened in March of that year, and since then Laurie and Kristin have been known as "the Pie Ladies."

But that's only part of the story. In August 2009 Oprah Winfrey was on the Cape for Eunice Kennedy Shriver's funeral. Kristin found out where she was staying and dropped off one of those chicken pot pies. Oprah fell in love with this savory comfort food. From then on it was "the Oprah Factor." She had "the Pie Ladies" on her program and at the end of the year added the Centerville Pie Company to her list of Ultimate Favorite Things. Business started to boom into the national market. A bigger kitchen and more production space became necessary. Then an arrangement was made with Cape Abilities, a nearby

nonprofit organization that provides jobs and services for people with disabilities across Cape Cod. Now much of the pie-making operation is handled by Cape Abilities. Laurie and Kristin donate a portion of their proceeds to the organization.

The Centerville Pie Company makes a variety of delicious pies. Popular fruit pies include traditional Apple Pie and local favorite Cranapple Pie, or there are savory pies like the Braised Beef Pie made with the Cape Cod Beer Company's Porter Beer.

CENTERVILLE PIE COMPANY APPLE PIE

(SERVES 8)

For the crust:

All-purpose flour for rolling out dough
1 double recipe of your favorite pie dough

For the filling:

⅓ cup sugar
3 tablespoons all-purpose flour
¾ teaspoon cinnamon
½ teaspoon ground nutmeg
6 medium Granny Smith apples (about 3 pounds), cored and sliced
1 tablespoon fresh lemon juice
2 tablespoons unsalted butter, cut into small pieces
Enough milk to brush top crust

For the crust: On a lightly floured work surface, roll out the pie dough to form two 11-inch circles. Fit one of the circles into a 9-inch pie pan, trimming to a 1½-inch overhang. Cover the second circle of dough with a dry towel while you prepare the filling.

For the filling: Preheat oven to 425°F. Combine the sugar, flour, cinnamon, and nutmeg in a large bowl and mix well. Add the apples and toss until apples are evenly coated with the sugar mixture. Add the lemon juice and toss again.

Pile the apples into the pie shell and dot with butter. Brush the rim of the pie shell with water just to moisten. Gently center the second circle of dough over the apples, pressing lightly around the rim so the moistened edge adheres slightly. Trim away the excess edge from the top crust and bring the overhanging edge of the bottom crust up and over the trimmed edge to seal. Crimp the edges of the pie decoratively with your fingers or with the tines of a fork. Cut a few slits in the center of the crust to release steam and brush with a little milk.

Place the pie on a baking sheet and bake 15 to 20 minutes. Reduce oven temperature to 350°F, and continue baking until the crust is lightly browned and the apples are tender when poked through the slits, 25 to 30 minutes more. Serve warm or cold.

CRANBERRY BOG HARVEST

Each fall, sometime between October and November, you can drive around Cape Cod and see cranberries being harvested. It is spectacular to witness the red sea of cranberries against a backdrop of blue water, sky, and fall foliage. The harvest starts with the flooding of the bogs where cranberries grow. This happens for a day or so, and then the actual harvest begins. In the beginning the cranberries were harvested by laborers with scoops (see photo of old scoop, next page). Today the berries are usually corralled and contained in a selected area (see photo) then harvested by machine and loaded onto trucks.

The cranberry, Concord grape, and blueberry are native to North America, and the cranberry is found only in the northern part of the country. Native Americans discovered the cranberry first; they used them as food, as a healing agent, and also for a dye. When the Pilgrims arrived, they called the red berries craneberry because the pink blossoms that appear in the spring resembled the head and bill of the Sandhill crane.

For more information about cranberries, visit cranberries.org. This is the website for the Cape Cod Cranberry Growers' Association, which was established in 1888. It is one of the oldest farmers organizations in the country. There you will find recipes, harvest celebrations, and more.

Cranberry Chutney

Chutney has a variety of uses. Try a piece of cheese on a cracker topped with a dollop of chutney, or use chutney as the perfect accompaniment to boiled meats. This recipe was adapted from The Green Briar Jam Kitchen Cookbook (see Jam Kitchen, page 54).

(YIELD: 5–6 PINT JARS)

1 pound fresh cranberries, picked over
¾ pound Granny Smith apples, peeled, cored, and chopped
1 medium onion, peeled and chopped
1 cup brown sugar
½ cup raisins
½ cup cider vinegar
½ cup water
¼ cup candied ginger
½ minced lemon
½ teaspoon chili powder
½ teaspoon dry mustard
½ teaspoon kosher salt

Combine all ingredients in a large kettle and mix well. Bring to a boil, reduce heat, and cook until thick, about 1 hour or more, skimming the foam from the surface. Pour into 8-ounce sterilized jars and seal.

Cranberry Nut Bread

Claire Desilets (see Cranberry Bog Honey, page 96) uses honey for anything calling for sugar. Here is one of her recipes for a delicious bread, perfect for that afternoon tea break.

(MAKES 2 LOAVES)

2 large eggs, room temperature
1⅓ cups orange juice, room temperature
¾ cup honey
¾ cup brown sugar
½ cup unsalted butter, melted
2 tablespoons freshly grated orange zest
5 cups flour
1 tablespoon baking powder
1 teaspoon baking soda
1 teaspoon salt
3–4 cups fresh cranberries, coarsely chopped
½ cup chopped walnuts

Butter two 9 × 5 × 3-inch loaf pans and set aside. Place the eggs in a large mixing bowl and beat well. Add the orange juice, honey, brown sugar, melted butter, and orange zest; whisk or stir until thoroughly blended.

In another bowl, sift together the flour, baking powder, baking soda, and salt; add to the wet ingredients, stirring just until combined. Fold in the cranberries and nuts, and divide the batter between the pans.

Preheat oven to 350°F, allowing the batter to rest 20 minutes as the oven comes up to temperature. Bake the loaves until a tester comes out clean and tops are browned, about 50 to 55 minutes. Allow loaves to cool in pans 25 to 30 minutes. Turn out onto a wire rack and cool at least 30 minutes more before slicing.

Green Briar Jam Kitchen

the finest all natural jams, jellies & relishes made on Cape Cod since 1903.

CRANBERRY CHUTNEY

Cranberries, Apples, Sugar, Raisins, Onions,
Lemons, Vinegar, Ginger, Spices, Salt

Thornton W. Burgess Society, 6 Discovery Hill Road, E Sandwich, MA 02537
(508) 888-6870 info@thorntonburgess.org www.thorntonburgess.org

FIN

800 Main Street
Dennis, MA 02638
(508) 385-2096
FINCAPECOD.COM
Chef/Owner: Martha Kane

I first met Martha Kane when she was the chef at the Brewster Fish House. I followed her to her own restaurant on Main Street in Dennis Village. The building next to the famous Cape Playhouse and Cape Cinema was extensively renovated by Martha's husband, Jonathan Smith, a Brewster native, carpenter, fisherman, and oyster farmer. FIN opened in March 2011. The rooms in this two-story building are cozy and warm. The side door leads you directly into the bar, which is small but comfortable. If you choose to dine at

the bar, you will probably have Tina as your server. If that is the case, you will be well taken care of. There are two dining rooms, one downstairs and one upstairs. Each provides the perfect setting to experience Martha's focus on local contemporary seafood dishes.

Over the years Martha has cultivated relationships with local farmers and fishermen. She does most of her sourcing close to home and takes to heart the "Buy Local Buy Fresh" concept. When I asked her how she got into the restaurant business, she told me that she originally went to school to be an artist and has a Bachelor of Fine arts degree. "I worked my way through school by working in restaurants. It was there that the interest in food happened. I now incorporate and combine my art background into my food." This is obvious when you think about her concept and presentation of the items on the menu, which are creative and innovative yet not overly complicated. And her food is delicious. Try the House Made Oyster Chowder (made with Jonathan's oysters), the Seared Native Flounder, or her organic grass-fed beef (recipe opposite) and you'll understand.

GRILLED PINELAND FARMS RIB EYE STEAK

It was mid-February, a week after Valentine's Day, and we decided to go to FIN. The Rib Eye Steak was on the menu but a different version of what Martha did in this recipe. We ordered it and here is what she did: Yukon gold potato puree, caramelized shallots, which were sprinkled over the potatoes, wilted watercress and a red wine jus, not on the meat but a gentle pool elegantly designed around the inside of the plate. Wonderfully satisfying for a cold winter night! There are many parts to Chef Kane's recipe. You may choose to do the whole recipe but you also can choose to take sections and add them to a dinner you are creating. For example, make the garlic chips and place them over a piece of fish or chicken, use the vinaigrette for your salad or the fingerling potatoes as a side dish. Think creatively when it comes to the chef's recipes.

(SERVES 4)

For the garlic chips:

12 garlic cloves, sliced as thinly as possible
Milk
Canola oil for frying

For the vinaigrette:

1 cup veal demi-glace, warmed (optional)
¼ cup extra-virgin olive oil
2 tablespoons champagne vinegar
1 tablespoon freshly cracked black pepper
1 teaspoon kosher salt

For the potato salad:

1 pound fingerling potatoes, scrubbed
2 thick slices applewood smoked bacon, diced
4 ears fresh corn, shucked and silks removed
4 scallions, thinly sliced on the bias
2 tablespoons minced fresh chives
½ cup mayonnaise
2 tablespoons mascarpone cheese
1 tablespoon harissa (or other hot chile paste)
1 tablespoon fresh lemon juice
Salt to taste
Freshly ground white pepper to taste

For the steaks:

4 (8-ounce) Pineland Farms rib eye steaks
Kosher salt and cracked black pepper to taste

To assemble the dish:

4 cups baby arugula
2 tablespoons extra-virgin olive oil
2 tablespoons fresh lemon juice
Salt and pepper to taste

For the garlic chips: Place the garlic slices in a small saucepan and add enough milk to just cover the slices. Bring to a boil, then drain off the milk, leaving the garlic in the pan. Add enough fresh milk to cover the slices again; bring to a boil. Drain, rinse, and pat dry. Preheat the oil in a small deep fryer or cast iron skillet to 300°F. Fry the garlic slices until slightly browned and crispy. Drain well on paper towels and season with salt. Set aside until serving time.

For the vinaigrette: Whisk the demi-glace if using, oil, vinegar, pepper, and salt together in a small bowl. Set aside until serving time.

For the potato salad: Place the potatoes in a large saucepan and add water to cover by at least an inch. Bring to a boil over high heat;

cook until potatoes are just tender when tested with a paring knife, about 10 minutes. Drain well. When the potatoes are cool enough to handle, slice in half and place in a large mixing bowl; refrigerate until cold.

Meanwhile, place the bacon in a sauté pan over medium-low heat and cook, stirring occasionally, until the bacon renders some of its fat and turns crisp and brown. Using a slotted spoon, transfer the bacon to paper towels to drain.

Place the corn over a medium-hot grill and cook, turning occasionally, until golden brown and lightly charred in spots. Transfer the corn to a cutting board; maintain the grill temperature to cook the steaks. When cool enough to handle, cut the kernels from the cobs; there should be about 2 cups. Add the bacon and corn to the chilled potatoes, along with the scallions and chives, and toss gently to combine.

In a small bowl, whisk together the mayonnaise, mascarpone, harissa, and lemon juice. Add the dressing to the potatoes and mix gently until

thoroughly combined. Season with salt and freshly ground white pepper to taste. Cover and refrigerate until serving time.

For the steaks: Season both sides of the steaks with salt and pepper and grill over a medium-hot fire. Transfer to a platter and tent loosely with foil.

To assemble the dish: Place the arugula in a large mixing bowl. Whisk the oil and lemon juice together in a small bowl and season with salt and pepper. Toss the dressing with the arugula; set aside. Slice each steak and arrange on four dinner plates with potato salad on the side. Rewhisk the vinaigrette to blend and spoon some over each dish. Top with arugula and garlic chips.

WINE SUGGESTION:
Bordeaux. A French red Bordeaux from the Left Bank's Saint-Estephe is a classic pairing for steak. It has cassis, graphite and earthy notes with enough ample tannins to make it a great wine to quaff with juicy seared beef.

Lemon Tart with Fresh Berries

(MAKES 8 INDIVIDUAL TARTS)

For the tart dough:

1½ cups (12 ounces or 3 sticks) unsalted butter, slightly softened
¾ cup sugar
1 egg
2 teaspoons vanilla extract
3 cups all-purpose flour
1 teaspoon salt

For the lemon curd:

4 eggs
4 egg yolks
¾ cup sugar
¾ cup fresh lemon juice (from 3–4 lemons)
4 tablespoons (2 ounces) cold unsalted butter, cut in pieces

Fresh seasonal berries, washed and patted dry

For the tart dough: Cream the butter and sugar together in the bowl of a standing electric mixer until light and fluffy. Add the egg and vanilla; beat until completely incorporated. Gradually add the flour and salt, mixing until the dough forms a ball. Divide the dough in half and wrap each half in plastic wrap. Refrigerate 15 minutes.

Roll out half of the dough on a lightly floured work surface to ¼-inch thickness. Cut four circles from the dough, each 5 inches in diameter, and fit them into four 4½-inch tart pans with removable bottoms. Repeat with the remaining dough to make 4 more tart shells. Place the tarts on a baking sheet and refrigerate until firm, 10 to 15 minutes. Preheat oven to 350°F. Bake the tart shells on the baking sheet until golden brown, 15 to 20 minutes. Cool tart shells completely before removing from the pans.

For the lemon curd: Whisk together the eggs, egg yolks, and sugar in a shallow stainless steel bowl until sugar dissolves. Add the lemon juice, mix well, and place the bowl over a saucepan of simmering water. (The bowl should not touch the water.) Whisk constantly until the mixture thickens and wisps of steam just begin to rise; do not overcook or the eggs will curdle. Remove the bowl from heat and whisk in the butter. Strain the curd into a clean bowl, press plastic wrap against the surface, and vent the plastic wrap in several places with the point of a knife. Refrigerate until cold.

To assemble the dish: Place each tart shell on a dessert plate and neatly spoon some lemon curd into each one. Decorate artfully with berries.

FOUR SEAS ICE CREAM

360 SOUTH MAIN STREET
CENTERVILLE, MA 02632
(508) 775-1394
FOURSEASICECREAM.COM
OWNERS: DOUGLAS AND PEGGY WARREN

What is a summer vacation on a hot summer evening without a dripping cone of your favorite ice cream? And where is the best place to get that cone? Anyone vacationing on Cape Cod between May and September knows that a trip to Four Seas Ice Cream on a warm summer night is a must. Order your cone or a sundae, stand outside the store with the locals and other vacationers, and enjoy.

The character, look, and feel of Four Seas has been the same for decades. Once a blacksmith shop, it is now quintessential old Cape Cod. The original wood floors slant,

and on the walls are old 4 SEAS license plates, framed group pictures of high school students who've worked in the shop, and the original black pegboards with the ice cream flavors that are available—or not—that day. The ice cream is homemade, and the selection is filled with old favorites: black raspberry, cookie dough, peanut butter chocolate chip, frozen pudding, pistachio, coconut, ginger, and coffee. Make sure you try their famous peach ice cream. This is the ice cream that Jackie Kennedy Onassis ordered for daughter Caroline's wedding.

During lunchtime grab a Four Seas sandwich. The lobster salad is popular, but you can also find peanut butter and jelly, cream cheese and olive, egg salad, ham and cheese, and other classic selections.

This famous Cape Cod institution in Centerville was founded in 1934 and got its name from the original owner, W. Wells Watson. The "Four Seas" are the four bodies of water that surround the Cape: the Atlantic Ocean, Buzzards Bay, Cape Cod Bay, and Nantucket Sound. In 1960 Dick Warren, a Barnstable High school teacher, bought the shop and operated it until 2001, when he sold it to his son and daughter-in-law, Doug and Peggy. Make sure to stop by this Cape Cod tradition.

PEACH ICE CREAM

This would be a great ice cream to serve with Dunbar Tea Shop's Bumbleberry Pie (page 40) or Twenty-Eight Atlantic's Apple Tarte Tatin (page 181).

(MAKES ABOUT 1 QUART)

For the fruit:

1 pound (about 3 medium large) fresh ripe peaches, washed and pitted
1¼ cups sugar, divided
1 tablespoon fresh lemon juice
¼ teaspoon almond extract

For the custard:

1 cup whole milk
3 egg yolks
2 cups heavy cream

For the fruit: Slice the peaches with the skin on; they should yield about 2 cups slices. Place peaches in a food processor along with ¼ cup sugar, lemon juice, and almond extract. Pulse 8 to 10 times to chop the peaches, leaving some small chunks. Set aside.

For the custard: Place about 1 cup ice cubes in a shallow metal bowl and place another metal bowl on top. Rest a fine sieve in the top bowl, and set aside. In the top of a double boiler, whisk the remaining 1 cup sugar, milk, and egg yolks until frothy. Place the pan over simmering water and cook, stirring constantly, until the mixture thickens enough to coat the back of a spoon and wisps of steam begin to form, 10 to 15 minutes. (Do not let the mixture boil or it will curdle.) Remove from heat and strain the custard into a bowl. Stir in the heavy cream, cover the custard bowl with plastic wrap, and refrigerate until very cold, 4 to 24 hours.

To assemble the dish: Pour the custard into an ice cream maker and freeze according to the manufacturer's directions. Halfway through the churning process, add the peaches and continue to churn as directed. Transfer to a freezer container; the ice cream will be very soft. Place the container in the freezer for 2 to 4 hours to firm up before serving.

Good Butter Bakery

239 Main Street (around the corner on Pleasant)
Hyannis, MA 02601
(508) 827-7353
GOODBUTTERBAKERY.COM
Owner/Baker: Terri Horn

Terri always felt at home in the kitchen with either her grandmother making bread or her mother making chocolate chip cookies. Later in life she worked with the famous artisanal bread baker Mark Furstenberg in Washington, DC. "He was a big influence in my life, and I was able to get scholarships to study in Paris."

I first met Terri at local farmers' markets selling her now-famous Kayak Cookies. Terri's cookies started in Washington, DC, where she lived and worked as a pastry chef. In 1979 she gave up working as a pastry chef and dedicated full-time to making her salty oats homemade Kayak Cookies. They were a big hit, and the sale of the cookies took off in the nation's capital. Then in 2005 she moved to the Cape. "When I was a child, we came here for summers because my family had a place here," Terri says. "I love the sea, ocean, and outdoors and decided to move here and start a business." This is the dream of most people who summer and vacation on Cape Cod, but most do not last through that first winter.

After working a few places to get her feet wet, she took the leap and opened her own bakery in Hyannis in October 2012.

Terri designed her own bakery as a large, open industrial space. It is fairly sparse but was done with impeccable taste. Terri is a perfectionist and is dedicated to the quality of her products—not only with her famous cookies, but also with what she bakes and creates in her new bakery. The small counter to the left showcases her delicious breads and desserts.

"My real thing is working with dough. It is so tactile. I love the texture and could roll out dough all day long." At the time of this writing, Terri had plans to make some special items. "I will have fresh-baked breads, pound cakes, and rustic tarts all baked daily and will be doing lemon squares like the ones I did in France. You have to use the whole lemon ground. It gives lots more flavors." I asked Terri what her favorite are, "My specialty is anything with butter!" she says.

BRIOCHE ROASTED RHUBARB BREAD PUDDING

(SERVES 8)

1 loaf brioche, crusts removed and cubed
1¼ cups roasted rhubarb (cut into ¾-inch pieces)
1 vanilla bean
6 cups heavy cream
8 large eggs
1¼ cups sugar

Butter an 8 x 12 inch-baking dish and fill with brioche cubes and roasted rhubarb. Set aside.

Scrape the seeds of the vanilla bean into a saucepan with the cream and add the bean itself. Heat cream to a boil, remove from heat, and let sit for 5 minutes to infuse the vanilla into the cream.

In a mixing bowl, whisk together the eggs and sugar until well combined. Gently pour the hot cream into the egg mixture, whisking as you go. Strain and pour the mixture over the brioche-filled baking pan.

Preheat oven to 325°F. Put the baking dish in a large pan (a roasting pan works well), place pan in the oven, and pour boiling water into the pan until it reaches halfway up the sides of the baking dish. Bake until the custard is set, about 40 to 45 minutes; test for doneness with a small sharp knife. Remove from oven and let cool.

Refrigerate bread pudding if not eating the same day. Serve with Strawberry Rhubarb Butter Sauce (below).

STRAWBERRY RHUBARB BUTTER SAUCE

(MAKES ABOUT 3 CUPS)

2 cups strawberries, sliced
1 cup chopped rhubarb
¾–1 cup sugar, depending on the ripeness
   of the strawberries
½ vanilla bean, scraped
½ teaspoon lemon juice
2 tablespoons butter

Combine all ingredients except butter in a saucepan and cook just until sugar is dissolved and mixture begins to bubble.

Remove from heat and stir in the butter. Strain and chill.

ROSEMARY BREAD STICKS

(MAKES 2 DOZEN BREAD STICKS)

1 cup plus 2 tablespoons lukewarm water
1¾ teaspoons dry yeast
5 tablespoons extra-virgin olive oil
3½ tablespoons soft butter
4 cups flour
2 teaspoons sea salt
8 tablespoons chopped rosemary

Put the water in medium-size bowl and add the
yeast. Let rest for 5 minutes.

Add the rest of ingredients, except the rosemary.
Mix until the flour is almost incorporated. Put
dough onto lightly floured surface and knead for
about 5 to 7 minutes. If dough is sticky to touch,
add a few tablespoons of flour, a little at a time, to
create a firm dough. Make a ball with the dough
and place in a warm, lightly oiled bowl; cover and
let rest in a warm place for 1 hour.

Place risen dough on lightly floured surface and
gently stretch into a rectangular shape. Divide the
dough into about 1¼-ounce portions and place
on a large surface or a sheet pan. Cover with
plastic wrap and let rest for 15 minutes.

Roll out each piece to about 15 inches long.
Before placing on a sheet pan, bread sticks can
be rolled in a sheet pan covered with semolina
and/or sea salt and rosemary. Bread sticks are
ready to bake after rolling.

Bake bread sticks at 375°F for about 20 minutes
or until golden brown.

The Island Merchant

302 Main Street
Hyannis, MA 02601
(508) 771-1337
THEISLANDMERCHANT.COM
OWNERS: BEV AND JOE DUNN
CHEF: JOE DUNN

The Island Merchant on Main Street in Hyannis features live music, good food, and drinks. It's part of a little empire built by Bev and Joe Dunn. This empire consists of three restaurants. The Island Merchant is in Hyannis, and the Islander is located at the Crosby Boat Yard in Osterville. Summer Stock, their latest venture, is in Dennis. It shares the grounds of the Cape Cinema, the famous Dennis Playhouse, and the Cape Museum.

The Island Merchant aims to add a touch of island flavor to a varied menu that emphasizes local and organic. You'll enjoy Chef Dunn's Caribbean fusion with a twist. The atmosphere is comfortable; it's the kind of place you can stop by for dinner or for a quick drink and a show. One of the most popular dishes is the $2 burger (slider) served after ten in the evening when the music has started. The music varies from jazz to folk, and you'll find natives and tourists having a good time. The Island Merchant is also available for private parties and can accommodate up to sixty-five guests.

You can also give yourself a treat and drop by one of the other restaurants. The Islander is a spectacular place to have a cocktail on the porch facing the marina at sunset. And Summer Stock is a great place for cocktails in the wine bar or dinner in the main dining room or the garden area on a warm summer night.

CAPE COD POTATO CHIP ENCRUSTED TUNA STEAK

(SERVES 4)

For the marinade:

½ medium onion, peeled and diced
½ cup orange juice
¼ cup fresh lemon juice (from 1 lemon)
¼ cup olive oil
2 tablespoons fresh lime juice (from 1 lime)
1 teaspoon cider vinegar
1 large garlic clove, minced
⅛ teaspoon minced Scotch Bonnet pepper
    or to taste

For the tuna:

4 (4-ounce) sushi-grade tuna steaks
Salt and pepper to taste
1 (7-ounce) bag Cape Cod Potato Chips, crushed
    as finely as possible

For the marinade: Combine the onion, orange juice, lemon juice, olive oil, lime juice, vinegar, garlic, and pepper in a bowl and whisk to combine.

For the tuna: Season both sides of the steaks with salt and pepper and place in the marinade, turning to coat. Marinate for at least 10 minutes and up to 20. Spread the crushed chips on a plate. One at a time, lift the tuna steaks from the marinade, shaking off any excess, and coat completely with the crushed chips, pressing gently so they adhere.

Grill the steaks over a medium-hot fire about 2 minutes per side (tuna will be rare), being careful not to burn the coating.

To assemble the dish: Cut each tuna steak in half and serve over mashed potatoes.

WINE SUGGESTION:
Provencal Rosé. Nothing says summer quite like a rosé from Provence. Choose a pale salmon-colored rosé which is elegant and dry as can be. The lighter colored rosés are usually based on Grenache and Cinsault, bursting with raspberry and strawberry flavors, along with floral notes and a good dose of minerality. There is enough weight and intensity of flavor to really showcase the magnificent tuna.

CAPE COD CRANBERRY BOG HONEY

Claire and Paul Desilets

FARMFRESH.ORG

Claire, an East Sandwich resident since 1948, was raised in an active 4-H family who lived adjacent to cranberry bogs. She kept bees as a 4-H project, graduated from Sandwich High School, and then went to college. That's where she met Paul, who was from Fall River, a city along the Massachusetts–Rhode Island border. They each have a degree in pharmacy. Claire and Paul married and settled in East Sandwich. They have managed over fifty hives on family-owned cranberry bogs since the late 1980s. (See recipe page 82.)

The Desilets are members of the Barnstable County Beekeepers Association and have held many positions of leadership. They instruct new beekeepers in the art and enjoyment of beekeeping on Cape Cod. When anyone mentions beekeeping on Cape Cod, the Desilets are the first names that come to mind.

DALLAMORA'S CAPE COD SALAD DRESSING

Lea Dallamora, Jon Mohan, and Reed Sherrill

DALLAMORAS.COM

In 2003 a restaurant in Orleans called LoCiero's closed its doors. While it was open, LoCiero's became famous for its salad dressing, so popular that it was sold to customers in empty wine bottles. After the restaurant closed, Lea Dallamora continued to make it in her Brewster kitchen. In 2012 she teamed up with her son, Jon Mohan, and his friend, Reed Sherrill. They found a manufacturer in Connecticut to produce the dressing, and they created a successful business packaging and selling twelve-ounce bottles. Dallamora's Cape Cod Salad Dressing may be purchased at Friends Marketplace and Phoenix Fruit in Orleans and at Millie's of Chatham General Store.

CAPE COD CRANBERRY HARVEST JAMS, JELLIES, AND PRESERVES

DEBBIE GREINER AND TINA LABOSSIERE

CRANBERRYHARVEST.COM

Their story began in 1995 at a children's play group, where Debbie and Tina became instant friends and, soon after that, great business partners. They started out making Ballerina Bunnies, but when an acquaintance suggested they make a food product, Debbie and Tina created their first homemade cranberry jelly. Now, eight children and many jelly flavors later, they are still friends, still cooking, and the proud proprietors of Cape Cod Cranberry Harvest. It has been an incredible journey for Debbie and Tina, and they look forward to many more years of friendship and jelly making together.

CAPE COD POTATO CHIPS

Lynn and Steve Bernard

CAPECODCHIPS.COM

Something that started out as a small cottage industry on Cape Cod has turned into a national success. Founded in 1980 by Lynn and Steve Bernard with no knowledge of the snack food business, Cape Cod Potato Chips has become a local institution and one of the biggest tourist attractions on the Cape. Steve originally owned an auto parts business. He purchased a potato slicer for three thousand dollars, and he and Lynn began making kettle-cooked chips in their kitchen. Over thirty years later they have developed many varieties of chips. They moved from the kitchen to a small storefront and then to the factory located at 100 Breed's Hill Road in Hyannis. Tours are given Monday through Friday from nine to five.

CAPE COD SALTWORKS
Janice Burling and Penny Lewis
capecodsaltworks.com

Saltworks on Cape Cod date back to the 1800s. At that time much of the Cape's industries revolved around fishing, whaling, and agriculture. As the fishing industry grew, salt became the best way to preserve fish and saltworks sprang up in many towns on the Cape. Today refrigeration has replaced salt, but the tradition of salt making is being carried on by Cape Cod Saltworks. Janice Burling and Penny Lewis started this venture in their home and have now moved their operation to Cape Abilities Farm in Dennis. This artisanal, 100 percent, all-natural salt has no additives and is evaporated from the waters of Barnstable Harbor and Nauset Beach in Orleans. It can be purchased soon from the website or in specialty shops around the Cape.

JUST JARS
Judy Fratus, Program Coordinator
jfratus@monomy

Just Jars takes mixes for breads, cookies, and soup, puts them in mason jars with fabric-covered lids and attached recipes. These cleverly packaged jars are produced in the Chatham High School Special Needs Vocational program. Just Jars can be found in the Dennis Cape Abilities Farm Shop and the Cape Abilities Farm to Table Shop, which is located in Chatham's Historical District on the road to the Chatham Lighthouse. The shop is also staffed by students from Chatham High School and carries other local products.

Naked Oyster Raw Bistro and Bar

410 Main Street (Pearl Street)
Hyannis, MA 02601
(508) 778-6500
NAKEDOYSTER.COM
Executive Chef/Owner: Florence Lowell
Chef: Julien Swanson

Owner and executive chef Florence Lowell has been in the restaurant business for some time. "For the past thirty years I have spent most of that time in the restaurant business. I lived in Austin and Houston before moving to Cape Cod eight years ago," she says. Five years ago she and her husband, David, bought an oyster grant in Barnstable Harbor. Florence grew up close to the Atlantic Coast of France, near Bordeaux, and spent summers in Arcachon, a major oyster-farming center. Becoming an oyster farmer strengthened her commitment to using local ingredients and brought back childhood memories. "It all made sense; now I could supply my own restaurant with these local, extremely fresh, tasty, and delicious oysters!"

When Florence and I spoke, she told me, "At this moment we have over three thousand oysters. Some of them are ready for market and the rest will be ready next year." Farming oysters is a delicate process, but the payoff is obvious in the restaurant's menu. After making your selection from the varied menu, you can choose to dine inside or, during the summer months, outside for people watching.

Florence's son Julien is now a chef in the restaurant. He's been working in restaurants since he was eleven, peeling vegetables at his father's Houston restaurant. "I spent a year in France at Biarritz at a culinary school in southern France near the Spain border," he says. He's twenty-six now and has been living on Cape Cod for four years. He's fluent in French, and, like his mother, has a passion for cooking. His Oyster Stew (see page 102) is a rich, wonderful treat!

CLAM CHOWDER

(SERVES 6–8)

⅓ cup unsalted butter
1 large Spanish onion, peeled and diced
2 celery stalks, sliced
½ cup all-purpose flour
4 cups clam juice (or part chicken broth or seafood stock)
1½ cups light cream
2–3 cups peeled, diced potatoes
1 tablespoon fresh thyme leaves
2–3 cups chopped sea clams
Sea salt and freshly ground pepper to taste

Melt butter in a pot over medium heat. Add the onion and celery and sauté until onion is translucent, about 8 minutes. Gradually whisk in the flour and continue cooking and stirring until no white flour remains and mixture just begins to color, about 2 minutes. Gradually whisk in the clam juice, stirring constantly to keep the mixture smooth, and bring to a boil. Add the cream and simmer until slightly thickened, stirring occasionally. Add the potatoes and thyme and simmer until potatoes are just tender, about 8 minutes. Stir in the clams, return to a simmer, and cook just until the clams are opaque, about 1 minute more. Remove from heat, season with sea salt and freshly ground black pepper to taste.

WINE SUGGESTION:
Russian river Chardonnay. Which is not dissimilar to a French Chassagne-Montrachet from Burgundy. It has creamy and toasty notes along with an intense and lengthy finish to support the butter and cream in this chowder.

Oyster Stew

Good Butter Bakery's Rosemary Bread Sticks (page 92) would be wonderful served alongside this stew.

(SERVES 4)

For the stew:

1 tablespoon light olive oil
¼ cup minced shallots
2 tablespoons brandy
½ cup sherry
4 cups heavy cream
24 fresh oysters, shucked, juice reserved
Salt and pepper to taste

To assemble the dish:

¼ cup minced chives or chopped parsley for garnish

For the stew: Heat the oil in a 2-quart, straight-sided sauté pan over medium-high heat. Add the shallots and cook until translucent, about 4 minutes. Add the brandy and quickly and carefully wave a long lit match just above the surface to light it. When the flame dies down, add the sherry, simmering to reduce the sherry slightly. Add the cream, bring to a boil, and reduce by half. Add the oysters with their juices and poach for 45 seconds; do not overcook. Season with salt and pepper.

To assemble the dish: Divide the stew evenly among 4 warm bowls, garnish with chives, and serve immediately.

NORABELLA

702 ROUTE 28
WEST DENNIS, MA 02670
(508) 398-6672
NORABELLA.COM
CHEF/OWNERS: JEFF AND EMILY WILSON

How does a forty-something-year-old Irish-German American open an Italian restaurant on Cape Cod and serve up some of the best American-Italian dishes around? That's a question many visitors to this charming and comfortable restaurant have asked. Other Italian restaurants on the Cape have been known to import chefs from Italy, but Chef Jeff Wilson easily outshines them with the dishes he produces in his tiny kitchen. Maybe it's because he always wanted to be a chef. "I was at my mother's side in the kitchen at the age of six," he says. "I loved being in the kitchen watching her cook. Later in life I had this passion to work in restaurants, and three years ago the opportunity presented itself to open my own place."

Norabella isn't the largest restaurant you'll find on the Cape. The restaurant has only ten tables, but the warm, friendly atmosphere gives such a family feel to the place you feel at home immediately. There are simple lace curtains on the windows, a chalkboard with the daily specials, and another one with wines of the day. It's the kind of place where you feel perfectly at ease asking the people at the next table, "What's that you are eating?"

Chef Wilson is extremely sincere, and this sincerity comes through in the food he makes and his desire to make his patrons happy. The menu consists of well-prepared traditional American-Italian dishes, such as Pasta e Fagioli, Eggplant Rollatini, and homemade Ricotta Gnocchi. The Penne Bolognese, Lasagna, Chicken or Veal Marsala, and Jeff's Tuscan Veal Chop (opposite) are customer favorites.

Tuscan Veal Chop with Pancetta & Cannelloni Beans

Accompaniments suggested by chef Wilson for this dish: mashed potatoes, sautéed spinach, and grilled asparagus.

(SERVE 2)

For the roasted garlic:

1 head garlic, excess papery skin removed
   (or ½ cup peeled cloves)
½ cup olive oil

For the veal chops:

2 (12-ounce) center cut veal chops
Salt and pepper to taste

For the beans:

1 teaspoon olive oil
2 tablespoons diced pancetta
2 teaspoons chopped garlic
2 teaspoons chopped shallot
½ cup white wine
½ cup chicken stock
1 tablespoon roasted garlic paste (roast before hand)
Pinch chopped fresh thyme leaves
Pinch chopped fresh sage
Pinch chopped fresh parsley
⅓ cup canned cannelloni beans, rinsed and drained
1 generous tablespoon cold unsalted butter

For the roasted garlic: Preheat oven to 350°F. Separate the garlic into cloves, and place in a small, ovenproof saucepan or baking dish. Add olive oil to cover and bake for 45 minutes to 1 hour, until the garlic is golden brown and tender. Remove from oven and pour the garlic oil into a separate container to save for another use. When the garlic is cool enough to handle, squeeze the cloves from their skins into a bowl, mashing to form a paste. Set aside.

For the veal chops: Season both sides of the chops with salt and pepper and grill over a medium-hot fire for about 8 to 10 minutes per side, to an internal temperature of 135°F to 140°F. Transfer the chops to a platter and tent loosely with foil.

For the beans: While the chops are cooking, heat the olive oil and pancetta in a medium-size sauté pan over medium heat. Cook, stirring occasionally, until the pancetta renders some of its fat and starts to crisp, approximately 5 to 10 minutes. Raise the heat to medium-high and add the garlic and shallots, stirring often until the garlic just begins to brown. Immediately add the wine to the pan and simmer to reduce by half. Add the chicken stock, roasted garlic paste, thyme, and sage and reduce by half again. Stir in the parsley and beans and heat through. Remove from heat and stir in the butter to thicken the sauce.

To assemble the dish: Place each grilled chop on a warm dinner plate and divide the beans and sauce on top. Serve with mashed potatoes, sautéed spinach, and grilled asparagus.

WINE SUGGESTION:
Dolcetto. This impossibly delicious Italian red wine is fresh, supple and dry with full dark fruit flavors and a seductive aromatic bouquet. The veal chop will be absolutely ecstatic with this giddy pairing.

Pain D'Avignon

15 Hinckley Road
Hyannis, MA 02601
(508) 778-8588
paindavignon.com
Owners: Vojin Vujoesevic and Toma Stamenkovi
Executive Chef: Matthew Tropeano

In 1992 four young men from Yugoslavia arrived in the United States looking for a better life. They wound up on Cape Cod and opened a small bakery in an alley off Main Street in Hyannis. They called it Pain D'Avignon. Two of the friends missed city life and left the Cape to open a bakery in Queens, New York. The remaining two relocated Pain D'Avignon to Hinckley Road near the Hyannis Airport and added a cafe. Now visitors can peer into the industrial bakery to see Pain D'Avignon's breads and other specialties being baked and cooled on large bakers' racks while having dinner or lunch at the attached restaurant and cafe—Boulangerie. It is a happening place year-round especially if you are dining at the bar. In warmer weather there are tables outside for enjoying a balmy Cape Cod evening of casual dining. It is also a great place to grab a bite when heading to or returning from the islands either by plane or boat. It is definitely a place not to be missed if looking for a place to dine on the mid-Cape.

Chicken Paillard

This chicken dish of Swiss chard and mushrooms uses local ingredients from Miss Scarlett's Blue Ribbon Farm in Yarmouth Port (page 161). It is the creation of the two former chefs, Toby Hill and Rebecca Arnold. The chicken is sautéed, topped with the vegetables and pan juices. A perfect simple comfort food on a French classic.

(SERVES 4)

For the chicken:

4 boneless chicken breasts, with skin
Salt and pepper to taste
1 cup grape seed or canola oil
Rice flour for dredging

For the vegetables:

2 bunches Swiss chard, washed well and patted dry
2 tablespoons olive oil
1 quart shitake mushrooms, stems discarded and
    caps thinly sliced
¼ cup chicken stock
Salt and pepper to taste or pinch crushed red pepper
    flakes (optional)

Transfer the crispy chicken skins to a paper towel to drain and cool; set aside. Place the chicken breasts between 2 pieces of wax paper or plastic wrap. Pound to ¼-inch thickness with a meat mallet.

Heat ¼ cup grape seed oil in a large sauté pan over high heat until hot but not smoking. One at a time, season the chicken breasts with salt and pepper; dredge in rice flour, shaking off any excess; and gently place in the hot pan. Cook on the first side until golden brown, about 2 minutes. Flip and cook on the second side until cooked through, about 30 seconds. Make sure there is always enough oil in the pan to coat the bottom; otherwise the flour will burn.

For the vegetables: Remove the stems from the Swiss chard and chop them into small pieces. Chop or tear the leaves into about 4 pieces each. While the chicken is cooking, heat olive oil in another large sauté pan, and sauté Swiss chard stems and the shitakes until the shitakes are soft and the stems translucent, 5 to 6 minutes. Add the chard leaves and chicken stock to wilt, seasoning with salt and pepper or crushed red pepper for a little more of a kick.

To assemble the dish: Place 1 chicken breast on each plate, top with one quarter of the shitake and chard mixture, and lay a piece of crispy chicken skin on top.

WINE SUGGESTION:
Viognier. A medium-bodied Viognier with peach and mild honey notes with underlying herbal nuances and a creamy finish is delightful with chicken paillard.

For the chicken: Preheat oven to 350°F. Gently remove the skin from the chicken breasts and spread the pieces of skin on a small baking sheet in a single layer without overlapping or touching. Season with salt and pepper. Cover the skins with another baking sheet to weigh them down and keep them flat. Bake until crisp and golden brown, about 15 to 20 minutes.

Pizza Barbone

390 Main Street
Hyannis, MA 02601
(508) 957-2377
PIZZABARBONE.COM
Owner/Chef: Jason O'Toole

Jason O'Toole grew up on the Cape in Falmouth and has been working in restaurants since he was seventeen years old. O'Toole studied at the Culinary Institute of America in New York and worked with Chef Gordon Ramsey of reality television fame in London. After London he returned to Massachusetts and worked in the Boston area before returning to Cape Cod to start his own catering business.

The catering went well, but the real adventure started in 2010 when Jason attached a mobile wood-fired oven to the back of his catering van and Pizza Barbone was born. "We were hitting the farmers' markets, catering special events and public and private parties from Cape Cod to Boston and becoming well-known for our pizzas," says Jason. Things were going well but Jason wanted something more. " I have always had the dream of opening my own restaurant, centered around my pizzas," he says, and in 2012 Pizza Barbone arrived on Main Street in Hyannis. Because his catering and mobile pizza business was so successful, he kept the name Barbone, which in Italian means "tramp" or "vagabond."

The restaurant is simply designed; for seating Jason found and refinished some pews from a little church in northern Massachusetts. But the real showpiece is the Stefano Ferrara wood-fired oven that you can see from every seat in the restaurant. "It is made from rock and ash from Mt. Vesuvius, the volcano, in Southern Italy. Stefano Ferrara is a builder of handmade firewood ovens in Naples, Italy," explains Jason. "It is a functional piece of art and weights over six thousand pounds. There are only twenty-five in the United States, and I have the only one in Massachusetts."

Pizza Dough

For his pizzas, Chef Jason O'Toole uses flour imported from Antico Molino Caputo from Naples, Italy. Caputo flour is blended to have a far lower protein content, which allows the dough to stretch out and keep its shape much better than the all-purpose flour we are used to. It is also formulated specifically for high-heat baking. Caputo has been using this well-kept secret formula since 1924. The "Tipo 00" designation refers to the fineness of its grind. If Caputo flour is not available, make your own dough with regular flour or use a pre-made crust from your local grocery store.

(MAKES 4 [12-INCH] PIZZAS)

5 cups "Tipo 00" flour

2 cups plus 1 tablespoon warm water

1 teaspoon dried yeast

4 teaspoons kosher salt

Combine flour, water, and yeast in the bowl of an electric mixer fitted with a dough hook. Beat on low speed 2 minutes. Let rest for 20 minutes, then add salt. Beat dough again on low speed for 6 minutes; increase to medium speed and beat 2 minutes more.

Transfer dough to a floured work surface and divide into four equal-size balls. Fold each dough ball over itself to create a tight ball. Lightly dust a baking sheet with flour and place the dough balls on it, spaced well apart so they don't touch even when they spread. Cover with plastic wrap and refrigerate 24 to 48 hours, or freeze until ready to use.

Bring dough to room temperature before using. One at a time, transfer a dough ball to a floured work surface, working carefully to retain its round shape. With floured fingers, press the air from the dough, working from the center out to form a crust. Lightly pull and stretch the dough with floured hands into a 12-inch circle.

Corn & Bacon Pizza

(MAKES 1 [12-INCH] PIZZA)

1 unbaked 12-inch pizza crust

¼ cup cooked bacon

2 tablespoons roasted garlic puree

2 tablespoons caramelized onion,

4 ounces fresh mozzarella, thinly sliced

1 ear of corn, kernels removed

1 teaspoon fresh thyme leaves

2 tablespoons freshly grated Parmesan cheese

Pinch salt

Preheat oven with a pizza stone to 500°F. Place the pizza crust on a lightly floured pizza peel. Spread roasted garlic puree and caramelized onion. Arrange mozzarella slices and distribute corn, bacon, and thyme evenly over the pizza. Sprinkle Parmesan cheese over and season with salt. Gently slide the pizza into the oven, on top of the preheated stone, and bake until crust is golden brown and puffy, 8 to 10 minutes.

Margherita Pizza

(MAKES 1 [12-INCH] PIZZA)

1 unbaked 12-inch pizza crust

¼ cup crushed tomatoes

4 ounces fresh mozzarella, thinly sliced

½ cup chopped fresh basil

3 tablespoons freshly grated Parmesan cheese

Pinch salt

Preheat oven with a pizza stone to 500°F. Place the pizza crust on a lightly floured pizza peel. Spread the crushed tomatoes on the dough, leaving a 1-inch border. Arrange the mozzarella slices on top of the tomatoes and scatter the basil on top. Sprinkle with Parmesan and a pinch of salt. Gently slide the pizza into the oven, on top of the preheated stone, and bake until crust is golden brown and puffy, 8 to 10 minutes.

Sweet Sausage Pizza

(MAKES 1 [12-INCH] PIZZA)

1 unbaked 12-inch pizza crust

¼ cup crushed tomatoes

3 ounces sweet sausage, casings removed, cooked, and crumbled

4 ounces fresh mozzarella, thinly sliced

½ small red onion, peeled and thinly sliced

1 tablespoon chopped fresh oregano

2 tablespoons freshly grated Parmesan cheese

Pinch salt

Preheat oven with a pizza stone to 500°F. Place the pizza crust on a lightly floured pizza peel. Spread crushed tomatoes on the dough, leaving a 1-inch border. Distribute crumbled sausage evenly over the sauce and arrange mozzarella slices on top. Scatter onions, oregano, and Parmesan over the cheese and season with salt. Gently slide the pizza into the oven, on top of the preheated stone, and bake until crust is golden brown and puffy, 8 to 10 minutes.

LOWER CAPE

Atlantic Spice Company

2 Shore Road
North Truro, MA 02652
(800) 316-7965
ATLANTICSPICE.COM
General Manager: Linnet Hultin

Cape Cod is filled with unique and unexpected places to explore. The Atlantic Spice Company is one of them. If you are heading to Provincetown, veer off of Route 6, take a left onto Shore Road (6A), then take a sharp left up a small hill and you will be in spice heaven. The store has been around since 1994 and has over 450 different herbs and spices. You'll find specialty items like saffron, zahtar, and vanilla beans, along with any spice you might need to cook your favorite dish and any herbs you might need for herbal therapy. You cannot go into this store without buying a bag of something.

How can a spice company be so successful on Cape Cod? Linnet Hultin, Atlantic Spice's general manager, stays on top of the latest trends. Hultin is well versed in what sells. She has been with the store since it opened and trusts her instinct for finding new products. She skips trade shows and instead uses the latest cookbooks, recipes found online, newspapers, and magazines to find out what's hot and keep it in stock. And the store also has a large mail-order business that focuses on home cooks, chefs, specialty shops, and health food stores, both in and outside of the United States. "If it is a good seller in the store, then we add it to the wholesale business," she says.

There are other items in the store, such as colorful teapots, beautiful hand-crafted cutting boards, and interesting wooden and ceramic dishes that can be used for all kinds of things, from holding condiments at a dinner party to holding soap in a guest bath. If you have anyone in your life who is difficult to buy a present for, I assure you that you'll find something at Atlantic Spice.

When I asked Linnet for a recipe, she said, "I want to use as many spices from the store as possible," and she came up with this delicious Vegetarian Curry.

Vegetarian Curry

(SERVES 4)

For the curry base:

3 tablespoons olive oil

1 large onion, peeled and chopped

2 medium carrots, peeled and diced

1½ tablespoons minced garlic cloves

1-inch piece fresh ginger, peeled and minced

1 tablespoon ground coriander

1 teaspoon ground cumin

1 teaspoon ground turmeric

½ teaspoon cayenne pepper

2 cups vegetable stock

1 (15.5-ounce) can unsweetened coconut milk

1 tablespoon tomato paste

1 (3-inch) cinnamon stick

For the vegetables:

2 large ripe tomatoes

1½ pounds cauliflower florets

1 pound sweet potatoes, peeled and diced
(about 1¼ cups)

2 cups roughly chopped, washed, and dried fresh
spinach leaves

1 (15.5 ounce) can chickpeas, rinsed and drained

1 lime, zested and juiced

Salt and pepper to taste

To assemble the dish:

4 tablespoons fresh chopped cilantro for garnish

For the curry base: Heat oil in a large sauté pan or Dutch oven. Add the onion and carrots and cook over medium heat until onion is translucent, 5 to 7 minutes. Stir in garlic and ginger and cook for 1 minute more. Add the coriander, cumin, turmeric, and cayenne and cook 1 minute, stirring constantly. Add stock, coconut milk, tomato paste, and cinnamon stick and stir until evenly blended, about 1 minute. Raise the heat and bring to a boil, then adjust to a simmer and cook for 10 minutes until vegetables are tender.

For the vegetables: To skin the tomatoes, cut an X through just the skin on the bottom of each one and drop them into boiling water until skins loosen a bit, 20 to 60 seconds (riper tomatoes require less time). Transfer tomatoes to a bowl of ice water. One at a time, lift a tomato out of the water bath and slip off the skin. Chop the tomatoes and set aside.

Return the curry base to medium-high heat and add the tomatoes, cauliflower, and sweet potatoes, stirring to coat. When mixture comes to a full boil, adjust the heat and simmer until vegetables are tender, 20 to 25 minutes. Discard the cinnamon stick. Stir in the spinach, chickpeas, and lime zest and juice and cook until spinach is wilted and curry is heated through, 3 to 5 minutes more. Season with salt and pepper.

To assemble the dish: Divide the curry among 4 bowls and garnish each serving with chopped cilantro.

Serve your guest a cold one from Cape Cod Beer Company (page 72).

BREWSTER FISH HOUSE

2208 MAIN STREET
BREWSTER, MA 02631
(508) 896-7867
BREWSTERFISH.COM
OWNERS: VERNON AND MELISSA SMITH
CHEF: SHAREFF BADEWY

In the 1950s the building that now houses Brewster Fish House was a farm stand and was then turned into a gladiola farm. "I kept the original sign (see photo page 121)," says owner Vernon Smith. Vernon has had the place since 1982, when his brother and he ran it as a fish market. "We knew nothing about retail. It could have been a scene from the *Lucy Show*, but my intentions were always to turn it into a restaurant," he says.

The food is American cuisine that uses as many kinds of local produce and products as possible. "Cape Abilities in Dennis is a big player for our products, as are Tim Friary's Cape Cod Organic Farm in Barnstable and Ron Becker in Brewster," says Vernon.

Vernon and Melissa have always created a nice atmosphere in the Fish House. The service is friendly and professional and the food is good quality and comes out promptly and efficiently. Chef Shareff Badewy started cooking when he was eight years old. "I used to watch my mother in the kitchen," Chef Badewy says. "My father was from Cairo and my mother from Staten Island, so the cuisine was an eclectic mix in our house." The menu runs the gamut from seafood dishes to steaks and vegetarian dishes.

The restaurant does not take reservations, so get there early if dining in the summer months.

MONKFISH WITH LENTILS & PUREED CAULIFLOWER

(SERVES 4)

For the cauliflower puree:

1 (2-pound) head cauliflower, cored and separated
    into small florets
3–4 cups heavy cream
2 tablespoons unsalted butter
Salt and freshly ground white pepper to taste

For the lentils:

12 ounces (about 3 cups) small cauliflower florets
2½ cups water
1 cup split red lentils
¼ cup golden raisins
1 tablespoon unsalted butter
1 teaspoon curry powder
⅓ cup pine nuts
Salt and white pepper to taste

For the monkfish:

4 (4-ounce) monkfish fillets
Salt and pepper to taste
¼ cup canola oil

For the cauliflower puree: Place the cauliflower in a saucepan and add enough heavy cream just to cover. (Add a little water if necessary to cover.) Bring to a boil over high heat, stirring occasionally. Adjust heat to a simmer and cook, stirring occasionally, until cauliflower is very tender, 10 to 12 minutes. Use a slotted spoon to transfer cauliflower to a food processor or blender and puree, adding the butter and just enough of the hot cream to make a thick puree. Season with salt and freshly ground white pepper; set aside.

For the lentils: Blanch the cauliflower florets in boiling salted water for 3 minutes; drain and rinse under cold running water to stop the cooking. Drain again and set aside. Bring the 2½ cups

water, lentils, raisins, butter, and curry powder to a simmer in a large sauté pan over medium heat, stirring often. Cook until the lentils are tender, about 20 minutes. Add the cauliflower, pine nuts, and a little more water if mixture looks dry; stir well and cook until the lentils just begin to break down, about 5 minutes more. Season with salt and white pepper to taste; set aside.

For the monkfish: Preheat oven to 450°F. Pat the fish dry with paper towels and season on both sides with salt and pepper. Place a large ovenproof sauté pan over high heat; when it is very hot, add the canola oil, swirling to coat the pan. Lay the monkfish in the pan so the pieces are not touching and sear until the fish is deep golden brown on the bottom and moves easily in the pan. Turn the pieces over and immediately place the pan in the oven to finish cooking, 7 to 8 minutes more.

To assemble the dish: Reheat the cauliflower puree and lentils, if necessary. Mound some puree on four dinner plates and spoon the lentils beside it. Position the monkfish over the lentils and serve immediately.

WINE SUGGESTION:
Rosé. The meatiness of the monkfish, combined with the exotic spice of the curry, begs for a deep and dark rosé with plenty of dark berry aromas and dusty minerality. A rosé from Southern Rhone's Tavel can actually approach the depth of color in a red wine! It's easy to see how this fleshy and chewy rosé can hold its own with this savory dish.

CAFE EDWIGE

333 COMMERCIAL STREET
PROVINCETOWN, MA 02657
(508) 487-4020
EDWIGEATNIGHT.COM
OWNER: NANCYANN MEADS

When you walk down Commercial Street in Provincetown, make sure to watch for the flight of stairs that lead to the most popular breakfast place in Provincetown. It's on the bay side, opposite the old library, and right near Freeman Street. This flight of stairs leads you to a narrow covered porch, perfect for breakfast, dinner, or just a cocktail. Step into the building and you're in an airy loftlike dining room where you can enjoy everything Cafe Edwige has to offer.

Opened in 1974, Edwige was the place to go for breakfast for many years. Then, in 1999, owner Nancyann Meads decided to offer her chef the opportunity to create a dinner menu. Now you'll find daytrippers, vacationers, and locals here morning and night. The staff is friendly, unpretentious, and talented. Every year they create the most amazing floats and costumes for the annual Carnival parade in August. And, of course, the food is divine.

Nancyann was born and raised in Provincetown, as were her mother and father, and the restaurant is named in honor of her mother. Her father was a boat builder and finish carpenter. Nancyann is a charming, elegant lady who has created a family-like atmosphere in the restaurant. She says, "Growing up in Provincetown was wonderful! I started working here as a waitress in 1974 and did this for seventeen years. Then I decided to buy the place. Now I have been in business thirty-seven years."

Cafe Edwige is known for its signature drinks as well as tasty omelets and Lobster Benedict (below). The restaurant has a strong following, so try and get there early for breakfast or make reservations for dinner.

LOBSTER BENEDICT
(SERVE 2)

For the Dijon beurre blanc:

1 cup dry white wine, such as sauvignon blanc
¼ cup sliced shallots
2 tablespoons champagne vinegar
1 tablespoon Dijon mustard
Zest from 1 lemon, plus 2 tablespoons juice

2 sprigs fresh thyme
1 bay leaf
¼ cup heavy cream
1 cup (8 ounces) cold unsalted butter, cut in cubes
Pinch sea salt

To assemble the dish:

2 slices Portuguese bread, or any other freshly
   baked bread
¼ cup unsalted butter
2 tablespoons fresh lemon juice (from 1 lemon)
1½ cups fresh cooked lobster meat,
   cut in bite-size pieces
2 poached eggs
1 tablespoon minced fresh chives

For the Dijon beurre blanc: Combine the
white wine, shallots, vinegar, mustard,
lemon zest, thyme, and bay leaf in a small,
nonreactive saucepan over high heat.
Bring to a boil, then reduce heat to low
and simmer until reduced to ¼ cup. Raise
the heat to medium and add the cream,
simmering until reduced by half; the liquid
should be thick enough to coat the back
of a spoon. Begin adding the cubed
butter, one piece at a time, whisking
constantly. Add each piece just before
the last piece has completely melted, until
all the butter is incorporated. Remove
from heat and whisk in the lemon juice
and salt. Strain the sauce into a clean
saucepan and keep warm until serving
time.

To assemble the dish: Grill or toast the
bread and divide between two serving
plates. Heat the butter and lemon juice
in a sauté pan and add the lobster meat,
stirring to heat through. Spoon the lobster
over the toasted bread. Top with the
poached eggs and a spoonful of Dijon
beurre blanc. Garnish with chives and
serve with home fries or field greens.

Try one of the Cafe's signature drinks for
your brunch.

THE CAPE SEA GRILLE

31 SEA STREET
HARWICH PORT, MA 02646
(508) 432-4745
CAPESEAGRILLE.COM
OWNERS: JENNIFER AND DOUGLAS RAMIER
CHEF: DOUGLAS RAMIER

The Cape Sea Grille is in an 1852 old sea captain's house and located on Sea Street just off of Route 28 in the heart of Harwich Port.

The husband-and-wife team of Jennifer and Douglas Ramier purchased The Cape Sea Grille in 2002, and Doug has been praised for his excellent fresh local seafood dishes. "I buy 99 percent local," says Chef Ramier. "I have fishermen in the area from whom I buy all my fish, and I use farmers like Veronica Worthington of Tuckernuck Farm in West Dennis, Tim Friary of Cape Cod Organic Farm Inc. in Barnstable, and Cape Abilities in Dennis for my produce. My philosophy is consistency and flavor first!"

Jennifer runs the front of the house in between caring for their two young children. The Cape Sea Grille has a cozy, comfortable atmosphere, and the service is friendly and professional.

The tables are far enough apart and not crowded. If you get a table in the back of the restaurant, you will have a little view of blue water. It is a perfect place to dine on a summer's night, then stroll down one block to the beach for a larger view of Nantucket Sound. Like most restaurants on Cape Cod, The Cape Sea Grille has a seasonal liquor license and is only open from April to New Year's Eve.

The Cape Sea Grille

Rising Stars in American Cuisine
James Beard Foundation Dinner
Chef Douglas Ramler
Friday, March 31, 2006

Crispy Oysters with avocado & pickled banana peppers
Seared Cilantro-Lime Scallop with potato crisp & sweet chilli sauce
Slow Roasted Pork Shoulder on a sweet potato biscuit with
crème fraîche & house BBQ
PINE RIDGE CHENIN BLANC–VIOGNIER   2004

Crisp Herbed Goat Cheese a top mesclun with roasted beets, hazelnuts,
orange segments & a caramelized onion sherry vinaigrette
PINE RIDGE CARNEROS DIJON CLONE CHARDONNAY   2004

Crispy Duck Confit served with stuffed Swiss chard purse,
roasted beets & Crimson Creek glace
PINE RIDGE CRIMSON CREEK MERLOT   2002

Sautéed Shrimp a top roasted butternut puree with smoked bacon, caramelized apple
& toasted almonds, finished with a spiced apple cider pan sauce
ARCHERY SUMMIT PREMIER CUVEE OREGON PINOT NOIR   2004

Pan Seared Lobster with pancetta, potatoes, grilled asparagus
& Calvados-saffron reduction
PINE RIDGE RUTHERFORD CABERNET SAUVIGNON   2003

Poached Pear & Fig Tart with caramel ice cream
R.L. BULLER MUSCAT, AUSTRALIA

31 Sea Street, Harwich Port, MA 02646
508 · 432 · 4745
www.capeseagrille.com
Chef Douglas and Jennifer Ramler

Oven-Roasted Cod with Autumn Vegetables

(SERVES 4)

For the root vegetables:

2–3 tablespoons extra-virgin olive oil
1 pound celery root, peeled and cut into
    ¾ × ½-inch rectangles
1 pound purple-top turnips, peeled and cut into
    ½-inch cubes

For the celery confit:

2–3 tablespoons extra-virgin olive oil
3 celery stalks, bias-sliced to ¼-inch thickness

For the cod:

2–3 tablespoons extra-virgin olive oil
4 (7-ounce) skinless cod fillets
Salt and pepper to taste

For the stir-fry:

1 head Belgian white endive, sliced lengthwise to
    ¼-inch thickness and submerged in lemon water
    to prevent browning
2 tablespoons extra-virgin olive oil
½ pound Napa cabbage, cored and shredded
½ pound shiitake mushroom caps, sliced to
    ⅛-inch thickness
1 clove chopped garlic
½ teaspoon chopped fresh thyme leaves
2 tablespoons chopped fresh parsley
Salt and pepper to taste

For the pomegranate beurre blanc:

½ cup white wine
½ cup cold unsalted butter, diced
1 tablespoon heavy cream
1 teaspoon fresh lemon juice
Salt and pepper to taste
1 tablespoon (about) pomegranate molasses

For the root vegetables: Heat 1 tablespoon oil in a large sauté pan over medium-high heat. Add the celery root and cook, stirring and turning often, until tender and golden brown, about 10 to 12 minutes. Transfer to a plate to cool.

Add another tablespoon oil to the pan and cook the turnips the same way as the celery root. Transfer to a plate to cool. Vegetables can be prepared one day ahead; cover and refrigerate until serving time.

For the celery confit: Heat the oil in a medium-size saucepan over medium-low heat and add the celery. Cook, stirring and turning, until the celery has lost its crunch but is not mushy or browned, about 12 to 14 minutes. Transfer to a plate to cool. Celery can be prepared a day ahead; cover and refrigerate until serving time.

For the cod: Preheat oven to 425°F. In a very large ovenproof sauté pan, heat the oil over high heat until it just begins to smoke. Season the cod with salt and pepper and lay fillets in the pan without touching. Cook until undersides are browned and move easily in the pan, about 2 to 3 minutes; turn and brown the second side. Place the pan in the oven and roast until the cod is just cooked through, 6 to 8 minutes.

For the stir-fry: While the cod is in the oven, drain the endive in a colander, tossing to remove excess water. Heat oil in a large sauté pan over medium-high heat. Add the Napa and cook, stirring constantly until wilted, 2 minutes. Add the shiitakes to the pan and continue cooking and stirring until mushrooms soften, about 3 to 4 minutes more. Repeat with the endive, and then add the celery confit, garlic, thyme, parsley, and salt and pepper; heat through.

For the pomegranate beurre blanc: When the fish is ready, place a piece on each dinner plate and cover loosely to keep warm. Return the hot pan to the stove over high heat. Add the wine, scraping the pan to loosen any browned bits, and reduce by half. Turn the heat to low and whisk in the butter, one piece at a time, until sauce is emulsified. Whisk in the cream, lemon juice, and salt and pepper to taste. Add the pomegranate molasses to taste; you may not need it all.

To assemble the dish: Place the root vegetables on a baking sheet and reheat in the oven alongside the cod. When hot, portion the vegetables with the fish. Divide the stir-fry among the plates and drizzle the beurre blanc over all.

WINE SUGGESTION:
Australian Chardonnay. An elegant Chardonnay from a maritime-influenced climate such as Adelaide Hills or Margaret River in Australia tends to be Chablis-like. Being bright and citrusy in nature with medium body and crisp acidity, it won't overpower the cod with all of its fixings.

CHATHAM BARS INN

297 SHORE ROAD
CHATHAM, MA 02633
(508) 593-4978
CHATHAMBARSINN.COM
EXECUTIVE CHEF: ANTHONY COLE

As you travel down the Cape, you find many treasures with a long history like the Chatham Bars Inn. In 1707 an affluent landowner, Squire Richard Sears, raised cattle and sheep on this property. He divided the land having twenty-five acres of waterfront property, and in 1912 a Boston stockbroker, Charles Handy, acquired the land with

the concept of building a hunting lodge for Boston vacationers. He built the inn with nine cottages that still stand today.

The inn has always been known for its food, especially seafood and New England fare. For the last six years, Chef Anthony Cole has taken over the kitchen and created new and innovative dishes using as much local produce and ingredients as possible. He told me about his new concept for the main dining room, Stars Steakhouse: "A cart of Midwestern grain-fed and dry-aged beef is rolled to your table, you pick your choice cut of steak, and then it is brought to the kitchen and cooked to your liking." There are also a variety of homemade sauces to choose from, like a red wine reduction and truffle foie gras, plus several gourmet sides like sautéed wild mushrooms, haricot verts, roasted fingerling potatoes, and caramelized garlic. Accompanying the entree are fresh organic vegetables grown in their newly purchased farm on 6A in Brewster.

Chef Cole went on to tell me about the extraordinary place they have for creating and enjoying a dessert after a meal: "We converted what used to be the chef's kitchen into a dessert lounge. It has comfortable cushions, couches, chairs, and tables. So when you finish dinner, you go to the lounge and can watch the chef preparing the desserts. There is a video camera and a wide overhead flat screen TV. We have a dessert called 'the Risk.' It is the chef's creation and changes all the time."

Besides Stars Steakhouse, there are three other restaurants at the inn: The Sacred Cod Tavern is open year-round, and the Veranda House, which serves lighter fare, and the Beach House Grill are only open in the summer months. They also cater special events and have pit-style clambakes that are a big hit during the summer months.

Cedar Planked Salmon

(SERVES 4)

For the vinaigrette:

2½ cups red wine vinegar

½ cup sugar

¼ cup red onion, peeled and sliced thin

½ shallot, peeled and sliced thin

2 tablespoons honey

1½ tablespoons Dijon mustard

3 garlic cloves, peeled and sliced

2–3 teaspoons kosher salt

½ teaspoon chopped fresh thyme

¼ vanilla bean, split and seeds scraped

Pinch ground black pepper

⅔ cup vegetable or canola oil

For the potatoes:

½ pound fingerling potatoes, washed and dried

3 tablespoons olive oil

Salt and pepper to taste

2 tablespoons unsalted butter

For the mushrooms:

½ pound assorted wild mushrooms, cleaned, trimmed, and cut up if large

3 tablespoons olive oil

Salt and pepper to taste

For the salmon:

2 cedar planks, soaked in water for 2–6 hours

4 (6-ounce) salmon fillets

4 teaspoons oil for coating fillets

Salt and pepper to taste

To assemble the dish:

2 heads frisée lettuce, leaves separated, washed, dried, and trimmed

¼ cup seeded, diced plum tomatoes

Salt and pepper to taste

For the vinaigrette: Put all the vinaigrette ingredients except the oil in a saucepan and simmer over medium heat until reduced by half. Transfer the hot mixture to a blender and, holding a folded towel firmly against the lid, puree until smooth. With the blender running, pour oil very slowly through the hole in the lid to create an emulsion. Set aside and keep warm.

For the potatoes: While the vinaigrette is reducing, preheat oven to 350°F. Toss potatoes with olive oil and season with salt and pepper. Spread the potatoes on a baking sheet and bake until tender, 20 to 30 minutes. Halve the potatoes lengthwise. Melt the butter in a large sauté pan over medium-high heat, add the potatoes, and cook, stirring occasionally, until golden brown. Season with additional salt and pepper to taste; keep warm.

For the mushrooms: Increase the oven temperature to 450°F. Toss the mushrooms with olive oil and season with salt and pepper. Spread the mushrooms on a baking sheet and bake until tender and slightly caramelized, 12 to 15 minutes. Remove from oven and keep warm.

For the salmon: Preheat a gas or charcoal grill to about 350°F (medium hot). Lightly coat salmon fillets with 1 teaspoon oil per fillet, season with salt and pepper, and place on the grill grate fleshy round side down. Cook just until dark grill marks form and fish loosens easily from the grill, about 3 to 5 minutes. Using a flat metal spatula, carefully rotate the fillets one-quarter turn, and continue to cook until more dark grill marks form, creating a crosshatched pattern on the fish. Transfer the salmon to the cedar planks, grilled side up. (Fish should not be cooked through.) Place the cedar planks on the grill with a little space on all sides for heat and airflow. Cover the grill and cook until fish is just opaque all the way through, 10 to 12 minutes. Transfer the fish fillets to four dinner plates.

To assemble the dish: Divide the hot buttered potatoes among the plates. Toss the warm mushrooms, frisée, and diced tomatoes with ⅓ cup warm dressing and season with salt and pepper. Arrange some salad beside each salmon fillet and drizzle everything with a little more dressing.

WINE SUGGESTION:
New Zealand Pinot Noir. Salmon has both high fat content and weight for a fish, so it requires a wine which is medium-bodied with good acidity. Pinot Noir from New Zealand's Central Otago or Martinborough fits the bill with its ripe red fruit flavors, fine-grained tannins, and crisp acidity.

Like many areas along the New England coast, Cape Cod claims to be the birthplace of the clambake, but the Cape's claim is said to be the strongest, because we are the first part of North America that the Pilgrims set foot on. There is a lot of folklore centered on the fact that the clambake originated with the American Indians. The Indians probably did steam and cook some of their food on heated rocks covered with seaweed long before the *Mayflower* set sail. However, if this is true, it was not the clambake as we know it today. In the book *Clambake* by Kathy Neustadt, there is a quote by Jim Baker, a historian with the Plimoth Plantation (March 22, 1988), that says, "No one knows much about the history of the clambake. There have been a lot of assumptions made, but we've never had to prove them."

Today the clambake is a big social event for native New Englanders and vacationers. It ranks up there with other all-American eating institutions, such as the backyard barbecue, the Saturday night church supper, and the family picnic.

During the summer months the pit-style clambake is the most popular, especially along the seacoast. Curiously, the celebrated clam (steamers or little necks) is not the star in this culinary extravaganza; it shares top billing with the North Atlantic lobster. The supporting cast usually includes potatoes, onions, corn on the cob (but still in the husk), chorizo, hot dogs, and sausage.

Sometimes chicken and sweet potatoes are added. The vegetables, clams, and meats are wrapped in cheesecloth and bagged separately for easy handling.

An authentic clambake starts early in the morning with the gathering of quantities of firewood and rocks the size of grapefruit. The wood is stacked and the rocks placed on top of the wood. The fire is lit, and the rocks are heated for several hours.

While the rocks are heating, a pit is dug. When the rocks are piping hot, about 450°F, they are tossed into the pit with a pitchfork. To generate steam, seaweed is heaped onto the rocks.

The food is then layered on the seaweed, sometimes in wood or wire frames. Food taking the longest cooking time goes on the fire first. The usual layering is potatoes, onions, lobsters, steamers, and corn. You can add chorizo, hot dogs, or sausage as the final layer if you like. It takes several hours for everything to cook.

Clambakes do not have to be large. Sometimes they can be prepared in barrels or new ash cans buried halfway into the ground to help seal in the heat. Rocks are heated and placed in the bottom of the barrel. Six inches of seaweed are added, then the food in layers. As mentioned above, food taking the longest cooking time goes at the bottom nearest the heat source. Seaweed is added between each layer.

Lobster Stock

When everyone has had their fill of lobster, save the shells and make a stock. It can be used in a variety of ways like lobster bisque—or add a little to your next seafood dish or one of your seafood chowders.

Left-over lobster shells
1 bottle dry white wine
Water
Onion, celery, carrot, optional

Place all the shells in a large pot and crush them with a heavy object. Add a bottle of dry white wine and enough water to cover the shells. You may add a cut up onion, celery, and a carrot but it is not necessary. Bring to a boil, turn heat to low and simmer for about 45 minutes, let cool, strain into small containers and freeze until ready to use.

Mini Clambake

Here is my version of a mini clambake that serves 4, using beer instead of water for steaming. It can be done in your own home, in your backyard, or on a stretch of beach over a campfire. You'll need a large kettle with a rack that will allow the food to sit 3 inches from the bottom of the pan. You can also use large stones from the beach. A good kettle to use is one used for preserving and canning.

4 small onions
4 small red bliss potatoes
1–1½ quarts beer
4 (1½-pound) lobsters (see Note 1)
4 ears corn in their husks
Steamers or littlenecks, about 1 dozen or more per person
8 hot dogs, 2 per person (see Note 2)
1 pound butter, melted, divided into 4 small bowls
Lots of cold beer to drink

Put the rack in the pan upside down. Put the onions and potatoes on the rack. Add 1 quart beer, cover, and bring to a boil; steam 5 to 7 minutes. Uncover, check to see how much beer has evaporated, and add ½ quart more if necessary. Be sure there is always at least 1 inch of beer in the bottom of the pan!

Add the lobsters, corn, and steamers or littlenecks. They may be layered over the lobster and corn or put into a cheesecloth bag. Finally, lay the hot dogs on top. Cover and start timing the cooking from the moment the steam escapes from under the cover. It should take 20 to 25 minutes for the food to cook.

If you are doing this at home, prepare your table while the food is steaming. I like to eat this outdoors. I cover my table with newspapers and have individual plates, nutcrackers, and small bowls for the butter.

There is no elegant way to eat this meal. Put on your old shirt and dig in. Dunk everything in the butter including the hot dog!

NOTE 1: See "How to Eat (or Deal with) a Cooked Lobster" on page 27.

NOTE 2: The grand star of this event is the lobster, but believe it or not the scene is sometimes stolen by the hot dogs.

PLACES FOR SUMMER CLAMBAKES (PIT STYLE AND STEAMED)

CHATHAM BARS INN

297 Shore Road
Chatham, MA 02633
(508) 593-4978
CHATHAMBARSINN.COM

The inn (see page 130) has pit-style clambakes from Memorial Day to Labor Day. They are family-friendly events that start at six o'clock every evening, Monday through Friday. There are games for the children and live entertainment. The evening ends with toasting s'mores by the fire pit.

CLAMBAKES ETC.

2952 Falmouth Road (Route 28)
Osterville, MA 02655
Jason Maguire, Sales
(508) 420-0500
CLAMBAKESETC.NET

If you are in the Upper Cape and decide you want a pit-style clambake, contact Jason. He will help you with the planning for a minimum of fifty people.

BACKSIDE BAKES

Nick Moto and Michael Silvester, Owners
E-mail: nutonic@aol.com
(508) 527 9538
Facebook: backside bakes
Twitter: @BakesideBakes

Nick and Michael do family-style, customized clambakes for as few as seven and as many as sixty people. They can do a complete party, including everything from a raw bar to desserts.

THE LOBSTER TRAP FISH MARKET AND RESTAURANT

290 Shore Road
Bourne, MA 02532
(508) 759-7600
LOBSTERTRAP.NET

The Lobster Trap has been catering events for twenty years—everything from weddings and rehearsal dinners to company events and birthday parties—and clambakes are their specialty. They cover Cape Cod as well as Southeastern Massachusetts.

PHOTO COURTESY OF THE CHATHAM BARS INN

DALLA CUCINA

404 COMMERCIAL STREET
PROVINCETOWN, MA 02657
(508) 487-5404
DALLACUCINAPTOWN.COM
CHEF: MICHAEL CERALDI
OWNERS: THOMAS PACILLO AND BERNABE OPRILLA

I first met Chef Michael Ceraldi at a fundraiser in Wellfleet. I was passing by a table he had for Dalla Cucina. He was offering samples of crostini rounds that consisted of a slice of polenta topped with a round of sausage. As I reached down to pick one up, he saw my name tag and introduced himself by saying, "Two years ago I read an article you wrote on cornmeal and the Dexter Grist Mill in Sandwich (see photo page iii), and ever since then I have been using the cornmeal for my polenta dishes!"

His restaurant is in a beautiful building with large pillars in the east end of Provincetown. During the summer months there is seating in front of the restaurant. When you enter the main dining room, to the right is a large, red slicing machine in a small section that looks like a butcher shop. Next to that is a comfortable bar.

Chef Ceraldi is one of the younger chefs working on Cape Cod, but he is quite knowledgeable when it comes to Italian cuisine. He brings a background of fine art and

creative thinking as well as a great deal of energy to his food. He studied art in Florence, was an apprentice chef in Bologna, and worked in New York City at Dal Posto, Mario Batali's lavish Italian restaurant. "I am Italian and try to keep true to my Italian tradition," he says. "I seek out seasonal and local ingredients to cook with. My pork and chicken come from Hillside Farms, Drew Locke's farm in Truro. I feed his pigs all our vegetable scraps. And because there are so many acorns on the Cape, I have been gathering them and feeding them to his pigs, like they do in Italy and Spain. All of my seasonal vegetables are from the farmers' markets, and my fish is from local fishermen."

CHICKEN LIVERS WITH POLENTA

(SERVES 4)

For the soffritto:

2 tablespoons unsalted butter

2 tablespoons olive oil

2 ounces sliced pancetta, minced

1 medium onion, peeled and minced

1 medium carrot, peeled and minced

1 celery stalk, minced

2 cloves garlic, minced

Salt and pepper to taste

For the polenta:

4 cups water

1 cup milk

2 cups Dexter Grist Mill Organic Polenta
  (or any stone-ground variety)

2 tablespoons butter

Salt to taste

For the livers:

1½ pounds chicken livers, trimmed and cut into
  1-inch pieces and soaked, if desired, in 2 cups milk
  for 1 hour (see Note)

1 tablespoon unsalted butter

1 tablespoon olive oil

½ cup Marsala wine

¼ cup balsamic vinegar

For the soffritto: Melt the butter with the oil in a sauté pan over medium-low heat. Add the pancetta and onion and cook, stirring occasionally, until onion is translucent. Add the carrot and celery and continue to cook until mixture starts to stick to the pan and vegetables start to caramelize, 20 to 25 minutes. Stir in the garlic and cook 5 minutes more. Season with salt and pepper; set aside. (Make the soffritto while the chicken livers are soaking, if desired.)

For the polenta: Bring water and milk to a boil in a heavy-bottomed saucepan. Whisk in the polenta in a slow, steady stream. Once all the polenta has been added, reduce the heat and cook, stirring occasionally, until thick, about 40 minutes. Stir in the butter and salt to taste. Cover and keep warm.

For the livers: If you are soaking the livers, drain and discard the milk after 1 hour. Dry the livers on paper towels. Melt the butter with the oil in a sauté pan over medium heat until very hot and carefully place the livers in the pan. (The oil must be hot to keep the livers from sticking.) Fry livers for 1 to 2 minutes, turning with a fork or tongs. Add the soffritto, Marsala, and vinegar. (Caution! The wine may ignite if using a gas stove. Never pour directly from bottle.) Raise heat to a simmer, stirring, until liquid is reduced and slightly thickened, 2 to 3 minutes.

To assemble the dish: Ladle the polenta into four warm bowls and divide the chicken liver mixture on top. Serve immediately.

Note: Liver can be soaked in milk for 1 hour prior to cooking. This will remove excess blood.

WINE SUGGESTION:
Italian Pinot Noir. A delicate and light Italian Pinot Noir is infused with Old World flavors of red berry, truffle and earth which will play nicely with the chicken livers and Marsala.

Hot Chocolate Sparrow

5 OLD COLONY WAY
ORLEANS, MA 02653
(508) 240-2230
HOTCHOCOLATESPARROW.COM
OWNERS: MARJORIE AND BILL SPARROW

In 1989 Marjorie and Bill Sparrow took out a loan and opened their first "simple candy store," as they put it, in North Eastham. Marjorie's love for chocolate started in her home kitchen, where she made all the chocolate sold in the store.

In 1991 a summer shop, the Chocolate Sparrow, opened in Wellfleet Center. "Two years later Bill built this building from a hole in the ground, and we opened Hot Chocolate Sparrow. It is a cafe version of the one in Wellfleet. We try to make candy for the masses and food and drink for the masses," Marjorie says.

The day I was there, Kathy Dufresne was making the toffee. "I have been making the candy for twenty-two years, and before that I was Marjorie and Bill's babysitter," she says. She was trained by Marjorie and now trains other candy makers here.

I watched Kathy make the toffee. "It is most important to use a candy thermometer," she says. "You can do it by eye, but I do not want to take the chance." She adds the nuts at about 270°F. She says, "I stir the mixture until it reaches 300°F, and then someone will come in and pour it for me."

Marjorie is proud of the shop she has created. It is now going on twenty-three years. "We are a great gathering spot for people in Orleans and the surrounding area," she says. "Because we are in the center of Orleans, it has become a meeting place for people of all ages, young and old. It is a place for people to come, hang out, and even work. During the summer months we hire a variety of different people; diversity is our motto, and my husband says we are like the United Nations. We have shared and taught a lot of people about coffee shops. We are the most popular place around."

Hot Chocolate Sparrow is the best candy cafe on the Cape, with lots of advantages like homemade special chocolates made on the premises, other candy, and good food and drinks. It is near the bike path and a great place to stop for a special treat. They are open at six thirty in the morning and close at eleven at night. They are closed just one day a year: Christmas Day.

ENGLISH TOFFEE

(FILLS 1 [12 X 17-INCH] PAN)

2 pounds butter
¼ cup water
4 cups superfine sugar
1 teaspoon liquid lecithin
2 cups chopped nuts, divided
2 cups milk chocolate, melted

Coat a rimmed, parchment-lined baking sheet with butter or nonstick cooking spray.

Melt the butter in a large, heavy-bottomed pot over medium heat. Add the water, then the sugar, stirring until sugar dissolves completely. Stir in the lecithin. Attach a candy thermometer to the side of the pan and raise the heat to medium high. Wash sugar crystals from the sides of the pan with a pastry brush dipped in water. Cook the syrup to 280°F, swirling the pan occasionally but not stirring the contents. Add 1 cup chopped nuts and continue cooking, washing down the sugar crystals again. When mixture reaches 296°F, quickly pour it onto the parchment-lined pan. When the candy is set, spread the melted chocolate over the surface and cover with the remaining nuts. When chocolate is firm, cut the toffee into squares.

Napi's Restaurant

7 FREEMAN STREET
PROVINCETOWN, MA 02657
(800) 571-6274
NAPIS-RESTAURANT.COM
OWNERS: NAPI AND HELEN VAN DERECK
EXECUTIVE CHEF: EVERARD ANTHONY CLEARY

"You are in a restaurant that was never a restaurant!" says Napi Van Dereck, owner of Napi's Restaurant. The restaurant was originally a property that Napi owned, which had a series of auto garages and junk shops that he rented out. And the property was also home to the antiques business that Napi and his wife, Helen, ran. "Whatever possessed us to open a kind of 'lobster in the rough' restaurant I will never know," he says. That was in 1974.

Since he couldn't get a bank to lend him the money he needed to build a restaurant, Napi decided to build their restaurant himself. Luckily, he was a carpenter and builder. With the help of other townspeople and a salvage yard in Quincy, his dream started to take shape. The "lobster in the rough" concept went by the wayside. "I'd lived in the Middle East and played the mandolin," he says. "We got a band together, played in the restaurant, and turned the concept into a Middle Eastern theme restaurant. Because we literally did not owe any money except to pay off the plumbers and people like that, we opened the restaurant and were able to survive. And actually made a profit that year."

The decor was determined by the antiques shop Napi and Helen had started, as well as by some old wood found at that salvage yard in Quincy. In addition, Napi and Helen felt the restaurant should represent the town and its many artists. Once you're seated, look around and see the brick mural done by Conrad Malicoat, the sculptures by Al Davis, and the paintings by local artists from Napi's own collection.

The menu has become more varied over the years and is now quite eclectic. The chef is Everard Anthony Cleary, known to everyone as "Tony." He serves up entrees and appetizers that hail from the Middle East, Brazil, and Jamaica. "I started here in April 1999. I'm originally from Kingston, Jamaica. I went back to Jamaica and brought my family here," says Tony. "Napi's is like a family to me."

That family feeling resonates with tourist and locals. The restaurant is open for dinner year-round, and does a nice lunch in the off-season. Stop by and feast your eyes and your palate.

KING'S FEAST

(SERVES 2)

For the tomato sauce:

2 tablespoons olive oil

1 onion, peeled and diced

1 large garlic clove, chopped

1½ cups fish stock or bottled clam juice

1 cup whole peeled canned tomatoes with juice

4–5 fresh basil leaves

Splash white vermouth

For the seafood:

1 (1¼-pound) live lobster

1 (8-ounce) fresh cod fillet, skinned

14 mussels, rinsed well and beards removed

4 littleneck clams, shells scrubbed of sand

4 sea scallops, cleaned and membranes removed

4 medium whole shrimp

To assemble the dish:

½ lemon, for squeezing

2 fresh basil leaves, sliced

2 tablespoons chopped fresh parsley

For the tomato sauce: Heat the oil in a very large sauté pan over medium heat. Add the onion and garlic and cook, stirring constantly to avoid burning the garlic, until onion is softened and translucent, about 8 minutes. Add the fish stock or clam juice, tomatoes, basil, and vermouth; adjust heat so mixture simmers gently for 10 minutes.

For the seafood: Meanwhile, bring a large pot of salted water to a boil for the lobster. When the water reaches a rolling boil, add the lobster head first and cook 9 to 10 minutes. Transfer to a shallow bowl and set aside. When the sauce is ready, nestle the cod, mussels, clams, scallops, and shrimp in the bubbling sauce and continue to cook until the shells open and the fish is opaque all the way through, about 5 minutes.

To assemble the dish: Transfer the contents of the sauté pan to a large, shallow serving bowl. Cut the lobster in half, if desired, and position on top of the feast. Squeeze lemon juice over everything and garnish with basil and parsley. Serve immediately.

WINE SUGGESTION:
Vinho Verde. Portugese Vinho Verde is an inexpensive yet delectable white wine that is bright, racy, and immensely quaffable. It has the ability to make shellfish even more mouthwatering. It's a steal for its price and this bouillabaisse will absolutely love you for it.

While fishing as an industry has changed on Cape Cod, there are still fishermen who go to sea and supply many Cape restaurants and markets with the catch of the day. I was shopping at Joe's Lobster and Fish Mart in Sandwich, where the canal meets the sea, late one afternoon in November. Joe's is owned by Joe Vaudo and has been in business for over forty years. It is one of the best places on the Upper Cape to buy fresh seafood. Scott Thayer, the manager at Joe's, told me something he thought I might be interested in. A fishing boat called the *Terri-Ann* was going to be docked in the canal, alongside the back door of the store, the next morning. "They will start unloading at eight thirty," Scott said. The next morning at eight thirty found me, photographer Francine Zaslow, and her assistant that day, young "Cody" (John O'Longhlin), at the dock to document this event. It was a wintry morning, the beginning of one of those cold, damp days on Cape Cod when the wind just whips off of the water. We watched as the *Terri-Ann* unloaded its bountiful catch.

Afterward we went into the store to warm up, and Scott told me that the *Terri-Ann* usually comes in weekly, depending on weather conditions. The boat, manned by the captain and three crew members, is out at sea about four to six days a week. "In a fifty-two-week year they make roughly forty-plus trips to us," said Scott. "The *Terri-Ann* just sells to us, but they are free to sell to anyone they want. Generally, when an offshore boat starts to sell to one purveyor, it is pretty loyal to that one. We sell most of the catch we get from them in our retail store, but some is shipped up north to exporters who send the lobsters overseas."

On my way home I felt so lucky to have captured and photographed this spontaneous experience with Francine and Cody. An adventure I could only have known about from being in the right place at the right time.

CAPE COD COMMERCIAL HOOK FISHERMEN'S ASSOCIATION

CCCHFA.ORG

The Cape Cod Commercial Hook Fishermen's Association is a nonprofit group started in 1991 by the local fishing fleet, who were determined to conserve marine resources through sustainable fishing. It has become the leading community fisheries organization in the region. In the travel edition of *Saveur* magazine, the association was commended for its work. The rules and regulations surrounding fishing on Cape Cod have greatly changed the industry and are hot-button topics down here. A visit to their website provides a great deal of information. The association also provides a variety of events such as the annual Hookers Ball, a fundraiser for the local fishing community.

BARNSTABLE SEA FARMS

LES HEMMILA
BARNSTABLESEAFARMS.NET

It was one of those beautiful September fall days on Cape Cod. I had arranged with Les Hemmila of Barnstable Sea Farms to photograph him in the waters of Barnstable Harbor where his oyster farm is located. Les told me he got his grant in 1991 and then started his business. He also told me a few interesting facts about oyster farming. "In the cultivation of oysters, the oysters have to be moved around at least once a month by stacking the racks and shifting them around. This prevents the oysters from getting a distorted shape. The oysters' shape has to be perfect in order to sell to raw bars. We want to make the most presentable product out there." Barnstable Sea Farms is a big proponent of the "Buy Fresh Buy Local" movement on Cape Cod, and their delicious oysters are featured by name at many local restaurants.

THE NAKED OYSTER

FLORENCE AND DAVID LOWELL
NAKEDOYSTER.COM

The Naked Oyster is a restaurant in Hyannis (see page 100). It's included in this section because it has its own oyster farm. Executive Chef Florence Lowell truly believes in quality, and when she learned she could farm her own oysters she went for it. "The town keeps all of the grants," she says. "When someone gives up or doesn't maintain his or her grant, then it is assigned to the next person on the list. You have to pay for the grant and abide by the rules of the town, and the grant must be properly maintained, environmentally. In Barnstable one can have up to about two acres. The grant must be renewed each year. And you must tell the town how many oysters you have harvested and pay a small fee."

BARNSTABLE OYSTER

KEVIN FLAHERTY AND TAMAR HASPEL
BARNSTABLEOYSTER.COM

Kevin Flaherty was a commodities trader and Tamar Haspel was an author. They were living in New York when they decided to make a big change. In 2008 they moved full-time to Cape Cod. Both can do their work out of their home, but they also wondered what else they could do out here on the Cape. Kevin became friends with Florence Lowell of the Naked Oyster. In January 2009 bad weather was on the way and Florence asked Kevin for some help with her oyster grant. Kevin pitched in and from then on he, along with Tamar, was hooked. He also met Les Hemmila of Barnstable Sea Farms around this time. Les was a real inspiration, and today Kevin and Tamar have their own farm and a distributor in Brooklyn. Their oysters can be found in many upscale New York restaurants.

PB Boulangerie Bistro

15 Lecount Hollow Road
South Wellfleet, MA 02663
(508) 349-1600
PBBOULANGERIEBISTRO.COM
Chef/Owner: Philippe Rispoli

PB Boulangerie owner and chef Philippe Rispoli, a native of Lyon, France, is bringing the taste of French country cooking to Cape Cod. Philippe decided to open his restaurant in South Wellfleet because he had vacationed there for many years. The building, once a small clam shack, has been turned into a delightful bakery and bistro. The aroma hits you as you walk through the door—that is, when you finally do walk through the door, because there is usually a line snaking down the walkway. Once you're in, you find a wall of beautiful fresh-baked breads and glass cases filled with delicious French pastries. The beamed ceiling in the bakery adds to the ambience. Past the bakery is a sixty-seat restaurant where the walls are covered with antique copper molds and pans. The bar is inlaid with shells and faces the open kitchen where Chef Rispoli works his magic. At the far end of the bar is a Limonaire, a hand-cranked instrument made of wood that produces music you would hear in the streets of Paris. Chef Rispoli says, "I brought it to Wellfleet to give my customers a taste of France."

On the day I was there, Chef Rispoli was preparing three beautiful country pâtés. He worked like an artist and, in his charming French accent, explained to me what he was doing. "I make everything from scratch, with quality ingredients. I lay the foie gras on top of the forcemeat and cook the pâtés very slowly." He then pulled the pastry crust over the long loaves of ingredients. On the counter he created a long braid to be placed down the center of each crust.

PB Boulangerie Bistro is well worth the trip down the Cape for that unique French experience.

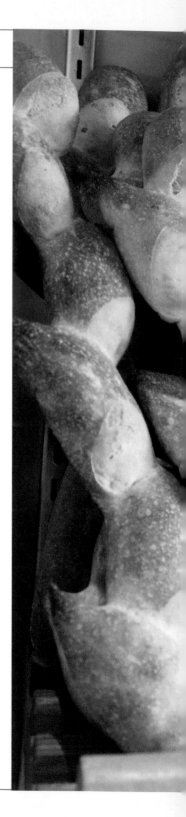

BRAISED SHORT RIBS

(SERVES 8)

For the wine reduction:

3 bottles (750 ml) dry red wine

For the short ribs:

2 tablespoons wheat flour

2 tablespoons malted barley flour

2 tablespoons salt

2 tablespoons black peppercorns, crushed with
    a mallet or the side of a heavy knife

1 tablespoon dried thyme

1 tablespoon garlic powder

¼ teaspoon ground cloves

8 beef short ribs (about 5 pounds), trimmed
    of excess fat

2 tablespoons vegetable oil

8 large shallots, peeled and separated and
    large lobes halved

2 medium carrots, peeled and diced

2 celery stalks, trimmed and cut into 1-inch pieces

1 medium leek, washed well and coarsely chopped
    and dark green leaves discarded

8 large garlic cloves

6 sprigs Italian flat-leaf parsley

2 bay leaves

2 sprigs fresh thyme

2 tablespoons tomato paste

3 quarts veal or beef stock

Salt and pepper to taste

For the wine reduction: Place the red wine in a large saucepan over medium heat. When the wine is hot, quickly and carefully wave a long lit match just above the surface to light it. When the flames die down, raise the heat to bring the wine to a boil. Continue cooking until wine is reduced by half. Remove from heat and set aside.

For the short ribs: Preheat oven to 350°F. Combine the flours, salt, crushed pepper, dried thyme, garlic powder, and cloves in a bowl; toss with the ribs to coat.

Heat the oil in a very large (8- to 10-quart) Dutch oven or ovenproof saucepan over medium-high heat. Sear the ribs until they are well browned, about 5 minutes per side, working in batches if necessary (crowding the pan will inhibit browning). As they are done, transfer the ribs to a plate and set aside.

Discard all but 1 tablespoon fat from the pot and add the shallots, carrots, celery, leek, garlic, parsley, bay leaves, and thyme sprigs. Sauté over medium heat until the vegetables are browned, being careful not to burn the bottom of the pan, about 8 minutes. Add the tomato paste, cook 1 minute, and remove from heat. Let mixture cool slightly, then transfer to a food processor and blend until smooth.

Return the pan to high heat and add about 1 cup veal or beef stock to deglaze the pan, scraping up all the browned bits stuck to the bottom. Add the rest of the stock, the wine reduction, vegetable puree, and seared ribs with their juices and bring to a boil.

Cover the pot and place in the oven to braise until the ribs are fork tender, about 3 hours. Bring to room temperature and then chill the ribs in the liquid overnight.

To assemble the dish: Remove the pot from the refrigerator and scrape off the surface fat. Place the pot over medium-high heat and bring to a simmer to thoroughly reheat. Transfer the ribs to a platter and boil the pan juices until reduced by half. Strain the sauce through a fine sieve into a clean pot, discarding the solids. Season with salt and pepper and return the ribs to the sauce. Reheat gently to serve.

WINE SUGGESTION:
Cotes du Rhone Villages. This French red from the Southern Rhone Valley is a blend of several grape varieties. It's a big wine with power and elegance, plus the added benefit of a long and juicy finish. A nice sensuous red to accompany earthy short ribs.

Pisces

2653 Main Street (Route 28)
Chatham, MA 02659
(508) 432-4600
piscesofchatham.com
Chef/Owners: Sue Connors and Ann Feeley

Sue Connors and Ann Feeley have created a charming restaurant with a cozy five-seat bar in the seaside town of Chatham. Wainscoting on the wall is topped with original artworks by local artists, and tables covered with white linen have parchment paper menus resting on them. With dishes like Pan-Roasted Chatham Littleneck Clams and Lobster Ravioli, it's clear that they have taken the restaurant's motto, "All good things come from the coast," to heart.

Sue and Ann opened their restaurant in 2001. "We started working together twenty-seven years ago in big hotels and then in smaller restaurants. Then we started looking for a place of our own," says Sue. "I was working in Chatham for a few summers when this place became available. Everyone said don't do it! But we did it!" They both come from conservative blue-collar families. "My family's philosophy is you do not give up a job with security, a weekly paycheck, and a job with benefits. My brother saved his bonus for when we went belly up." Luckily Sue's brother can keep that bonus, because Pisces has been a smashing success.

Chatham Littleneck Clams in Portuguese Kale Stew

(SERVES 4 AS AN APPETIZER OR 2 AS A MAIN COURSE)

For the stew:

2 tablespoons canola or olive oil

⅓ cup diced onions

1 teaspoon chopped garlic

Pinch crushed red pepper flakes

1 bay leaf

¾ cup sliced Portuguese chorizo

¾ cup peeled, diced carrots

¾ cup diced red potatoes, skin on

1 (24-ounce) bottle clam juice or lobster stock
(page 136)

1 bunch kale, washed, dried, stemmed, and leaves
coarsely chopped

½ cup canned cannellini beans, rinsed and drained

⅓ cup diced fresh tomatoes

32 littleneck clams, shells scrubbed in cold water
to remove sand

To assemble the dish:

Focaccia or other rustic Italian bread, sliced thick

Softened Garlic Butter (page 12) or olive oil

For the stew: Heat the oil in an 8-quart, straight-sided sauté pan over medium-high heat. Add the onions and cook, stirring, just until onions are translucent, about 5 minutes. Add the garlic, red pepper flakes, and bay leaf; cook 1 minute more. Add the chorizo and cook until it begins to release some of its oil, then add the carrots and potatoes and continue cooking until vegetables begin to soften. Add the clam juice or lobster stock, raise the heat to high, and bring to a boil. Stir in the kale, beans, and tomatoes and when mixture returns to a boil, lower the heat so the stew simmers until the kale turns dark green and is very tender, 5 to 8 minutes.

Arrange the clams in a single layer over the stew and cover tightly with a lid or foil. Let the clams steam until they open, 5 to 10 minutes. (Discard any clams that do not open.) Taste the broth and adjust seasoning, adding a little more water if it's too salty.

To assemble the dish: Use tongs to divide the clams among warm shallow pasta bowls and ladle the stew over them. Serve with bread for dipping, brushed with garlic butter or oil and toasted or grilled if desired.

WINE SUGGESTION:
Albarino. This truly exceptional Spanish white wine has citrus and apple notes supported by fresh, lively acidity. It has remarkable complexity that can easily stand up to the vibrant flavors in this robust kale soup.

Many of the local farms offer what is known as a Community Supported Agriculture (CSA) program. You pay a fee to the farmer at the beginning of the season, then pick up a box of freshly harvested produce on a weekly basis.

NOT ENOUGH ACRES FARM
107 Sesusit Road
East Dennis, MA 02641
(508) 737-3446
Owners: Jeff and Beth Deck

Not Enough Acres Farm sells hats, gloves, and bags, as well as vegetables, fruits, herbs, and honey. Jeff (shown below) and Beth Deck own Shetland Islamic sheep, and Beth spins and makes all the items from their wool. When the Decks started the farm, they didn't have enough property to get a tax break on their farm, so they leased the property across the street in order to get the necessary 5.25 acres. That's how the farm got its name. The Decks have now been on the property for thirty-three years.

CAPE ABILITIES FARM
458 Main Street (Route 6A)
Dennis, MA 02638
(508) 385-2538
CAPEABILITIES.ORG

There are two Cape Abilities Farm locations: one in Dennis, which operates a farm stand and the greenhouses, and another in Marston Mills, which is a working farm. All produce grown in Marston Mills is transported to Dennis to be sold. The farms provide paid employment for people with disabilities who work in all areas of farm management. The farm sells to many of the restaurants on Cape Cod, including FIN, the Brewster Fish House, the Chatham Bars Inn, the Naked Oyster, and Pain D'Avignon. Cape Abilities also has a number of business partnerships. The Centerville Pie Company is one such partner and now has most of its pie production done in the Hyannis branch, where over forty disabled adults are employed. Other partners are the Woods Hole Oceanographic Institute and Cape Cod Beach Buckets. Most recently Cape Abilities has been providing space for Cape Cod Saltworks to harvest salt.

CAPE COD ORGANIC FARM

3675 Main Street (Route 6A)
Barnstable, MA 02630
(508) 362-3573
Owner: Tim Friary
capecodorganicfarm.org

The farm is certified organic and specializes in fruits (starting with delicious strawberries in early summer), cut flowers, herbs, and vegetables into the early winter. Tim (shown right) also raises Heritage Breed Pigs for pork and has laying chickens for eggs.

TUCKERNUCK FARM

89 Fisk Street
West Dennis, MA 02670
(508) 364-5821
Owner: Veronica Worthington

Tuckernuck Farm was founded in 1998 on an acre of land. Veronica Worthington (shown left) sells her variety of heirloom lettuce, which she is noted for, at farmers' markets and her farm stand, which is open from the end of May to November. She also sells wool and wool roving from her heritage sheep. The farm also offers the CSA program.

MISS SCARLETT'S BLUE RIBBON FARM

555 Route 6A and Wier Road
Yarmouth Port, MA 02675
(508) 420-9748
Owners: Susan and Jim Knierien
missscarlettsblueribbonfarm.com

This is a family-owned working farm that provides customers and local restaurants with fresh, local produce, poultry, and pork. During the summer months and into the fall, there are vegetables, flowers, herbs, squashes, melons, and, of course, eggs. The farm welcomes visitors.

BUY FRESH BUY LOCAL

The theme "Buy Fresh Buy Local" is the slogan at all farmers markets on Cape Cod. Our season starts in May and continues into November.

Early spring farmers bring out many kinds of produce (or plants) they have started in green houses like lettuces, peas, tomatoes and many of the plants we use for our gardens, both vegetable and flower. For me, I prepare my gardens before hand and find it easier to buy pre-started plants rather than seeds I have started myself. I go to the markets, pick my plants, and have an instant garden by Memorial Day.

As the season progresses so does the abundance of fruits and vegetables in the markets. And don't forget lobsters, seafood, artisanal cookies, breads, jams and jellies.

When fall approaches, I look forward to the many variety of apples, pumpkins, and squashes. Each year I find a new variety of something I have not seen before.

CAPE COD
BUY FRESH
BUY LOCAL.
www.BuyFreshBuyLocalCapeCod.org

THE RED INN

15 COMMERCIAL STREET
PROVINCETOWN, MA 02657
(508) 487-7334
THEREDINN.COM
OWNERS: DAVID SILVA, SEAN
BURKE, AND PHILIP MOSSY JR.
EXECUTIVE CHEF: PHILIP
MOSSY JR.

The Red Inn is located at Provincetown's far west end. This charming establishment dates back to 1805 and has a long history of dignitaries and celebrities who have stayed here. President Theodore Roosevelt and Mrs. Roosevelt stayed at the inn when they came for the laying of the cornerstone for the Provincetown Monument in 1907. Over the years people like Joseph Kennedy and the Nixons had special rooms here. Gloria Swanson was a visitor here. She had her favorite artist, Ada Rayner, paint the mural over the fireplace in the room across from the bar. In fact a small dining room at the inn is named for Ada Rayner, who was part of the Provincetown art colony and married to Henry Hensche, founder of the Provincetown School of Art.

"It was a landmark in the fifties and sixties and fell on hard times in the mid-eighties and throughout the nineties," says David Silva, one of the owners. "The three of us bought it in 2001 and renovated and opened it in 2002. We brought it to where it is today. Over the years we have been very fortunate to have lots of publicity and lots more celebrities come and stay. Norman Mailer's movie was filmed here." Silva is a third generation Provincetown native. "My family owned the Dairy Queen for forty-five years, my grandfather ran the

bank, my uncle was principal of the high school, and I am very fortunate to own such a historical landmark in the town where I grew up."

For starters, try the Lobster Sliders served on two mini buns or the Seafood Sampler with oysters, clams, shrimp, and lobster tails. The main courses run the gamut from fresh local seafood to steaks, chops, chicken, and duck. One of the Red Inn's signature dishes is the Lamb Chops (below).

The view from the bar and dining room is one of the best on Cape Cod. Whether you're having a drink or dining, the ever-changing Provincetown Harbor, the lighthouse at Long Point, and the sandy cliffs along the shores of the Outer Cape are sights you will long remember.

HERB-MARINATED LAMB CHOPS

(SERVES 4)

For the marinade:

½ cup honey

¼ cup Dijon mustard

2 tablespoons minced fresh rosemary

1 tablespoon minced fresh thyme

1 tablespoon minced fresh basil

½ teaspoon salt

¼ teaspoon coarsely ground black pepper

12 baby lamb chops

For the marinade: Combine the honey, mustard, herbs, and salt and pepper in a medium bowl and mix well.

Place the lamb chops in a shallow dish large enough to hold them in a single layer. Spread the marinade over the lamb, turning to coat all sides. Let stand at room temperature for 30 minutes, or cover and refrigerate overnight. Grill or broil the chops to desired doneness, about 4 to 5 minutes per side for medium-rare. Transfer to a plate, cover loosely with foil, and allow to rest 5 minutes before serving.

WINE SUGGESTION:
Barolo. Barolo is a stunning Italian red, made entirely from Nebbiolo, with aromas and flavors of red cherries and perfumed roses, along with rich silky tannins. It's a classic pairing for lamb and a winner every single time.

Sunbird Food Truck

2520 Route 6A
Wellfleet, MA 02667
(508) 237-0354
BIRDINTHESUN.COM
Chef/Owner: J'aime Sparrow
Co-Owner: Christian Sparrow

One day last summer while driving down the Cape, I noticed a beautifully painted food truck in Wellfleet. I had to stop and investigate. This was my introduction to the Sunbird Food Truck, with its beautifully lettered motto, "Eat well . . . on the Fly," painted over the serving window, and to owners J'aime and Christian Sparrow. Christian is from Cape Cod, and J'amie is from Connecticut. They have known each other since childhood. J'aime's passion is food and Christian's is design. They spent ten years in San Francisco, where J'aime worked in the restaurant business and Christian was in interactive design and advertising. They moved to Cape Cod in 2010 and bought the truck. J'aime became the chef, and Christian was fortunate enough to bring several of his clients with him. He also hand painted the truck.

"We both have a passion for nostalgia and the salty side of Cape Cod," Christian says. "And, of course, the good, simple food that we serve in the Sunbird." J'aime has created a delicious, interesting menu, much of it using local ingredients. The menu is displayed on a blackboard propped against the truck. The day I was there, the featured items were a Fish Taco on a Corn Tortilla, a Gourmet Hot Dog (this is usually on the menu), and a Market Sandwich with fresh mozzarella and oven-roasted tomatoes. Most days you can also grab a breakfast sandwich with local eggs to order and smoked bacon. Pull in and order something "on the fly" or stay and eat at one of the nearby picnic tables.

SUNBIRD BRUSSELS SPROUTS

(SERVES 4–6)

For the brussels sprouts:

1 pound brussels sprouts, trimmed, halved, and quartered if large
Salt for boiling water

For the pecans:

2 cups pecans
2 tablespoons brown sugar
2½ teaspoons olive oil
2 teaspoons Chinese five-spice powder
1½ teaspoons salt
½ teaspoon crushed red pepper flakes

For the citrus butter:

½ cup unsalted butter, room temperature
1 tablespoon finely chopped shallot
Zest of 1 orange
1 teaspoon honey
¾ teaspoon ground cinnamon
½ teaspoon salt

For the pancetta:

1 teaspoon olive oil
⅛ pound pancetta, thinly sliced

To assemble the dish:

1 tablespoon olive oil
¼ cup cider vinegar

For the brussels sprouts: Blanch the sprouts in boiling, salted water just until al dente, 4 to 5 minutes. Transfer to a bowl of ice water to stop the cooking. Drain very well and set aside. This can be done a day ahead; cover and refrigerate until ready to serve.

For the pecans: Preheat oven to 375°F. Toss the nuts, brown sugar, olive oil, five-spice powder, salt, and red pepper flakes in a bowl until evenly coated. Spread in a single layer on a baking sheet lined with parchment paper and bake until golden and fragrant, 7 to 9 minutes. Let cool on a baking sheet, then roughly chop and set aside. This can be done ahead; store in an airtight container at room temperature until ready to serve.

For the citrus butter: Place the butter, shallot, orange zest, honey, cinnamon, and salt in a mixing bowl. Mash and stir with a fork until creamy and incorporated. Set aside. This can be done a day ahead; cover and refrigerate until ready to serve.

For the pancetta: Heat the oil in a sauté pan just large enough to hold the pancetta slices. When the oil is hot, add the pancetta and cook until crisp. Drain on paper towels and crumble. Set aside.

To assemble the dish: Heat olive oil in a very large sauté pan or seasoned cast iron skillet. Add the blanched brussels sprouts and cook, tossing occasionally, until browned, 3 to 7 minutes. Reduce heat to low and add a generous spoonful of citrus butter. Toss again until butter is melted and sprouts are well coated. Increase heat to medium-high and add the vinegar, tossing to distribute. Cook to reduce the vinegar, about 1 minute more, and remove from heat. Add about ¾ cup chopped seasoned pecans and garnish with the crumbled pancetta.

TRURO VINEYARDS

11 SHORE ROAD
NORTH TRURO, MA 02652
(508) 487-6200
TRUROVINEYARDSOFCAPECOD.COM
OWNERS: THE ROBERTS FAMILY

The story goes like this: Dave Roberts went out for a bike ride one day while vacationing in Truro and came home with a vineyard. Dave had just retired after a career in the wine and spirits industry, and operating a vineyard had always been a dream of his. "Cathy and I are from Connecticut and have been coming here since our honeymoon forty-seven years ago," says Dave. "This vineyard has been in operation since 1991, and we've owned it for six years. It's working! We have a good business plan, and we are making it work! Our whole family—our son and two daughters—are equal owners and share the tasks of the operation."

It is worth a trip here just to look at the beautiful setting of Truro Vineyards. The house and lands have been in existence for two centuries. Passed down through the Hughes and Rich families, the property inspired two paintings by Edward Hopper: Just off Route 6, it's a great place to stop for a tour and a wine tasting. The vineyard

has a wonderful pavilion out back that can host special events of up to sixty-five people. My favorite is the barrel room, where the wine is stored. The barrels line one wall, and the air is filled with the smell of fermenting grapes. On each side of the huge sliding wood doors that lead to the fermenting rooms are murals painted by Dave and Cathy's nephew, Mark Melnick. One is a map of Cape Cod and the other is of the whole family working in the vineyards. While used frequently for rehearsal dinners, I think the barrel room would be a great place to throw a party for any occasion!

The Roberts family has all bases covered at Truro Vineyards. There's the wine, the wine and gift store, tours, places for events, the sweeping view of the vineyards, and the beautifully manicured estate. This is a unique and different place on Cape Cod.

DAVE'S CHEESEBURGERS

(SERVES 4)

2 pounds ground beef (85% lean and 15% fat)

1 teaspoon olive oil

1 teaspoon Worcestershire sauce

Pinch sea salt

Pinch steak seasoning (Canadian mix works well)

½ teaspoon garlic flakes

4 slices American cheese or your favorite cheese

4 hamburger buns

Place the ground beef in a large bowl along with the next 5 ingredients (through garlic flakes). Mix gently by hand to combine, taking care not to compress the ingredients. Shape the meat into four and only four thick patties. Start grilling on a hot grill to sear both sides, then cook to medium-rare on medium heat, adding cheese and covering 2 minutes before done. Serve on hamburger buns.

DAVE'S FAMOUS ONION/BLUE CHEESE TOPPING

¼ stick (2 tablespoons) butter

2 tablespoons olive oil

1–3 onions, depending on size

4 cloves garlic, chopped

¼ cup red wine (Truro Vineyards Cabernet Franc), or your favorite Cabernet Franc if not available.

Pinch Italian mixed seasonings

¼ pound blue cheese

Heat a cast iron skillet on medium-high heat. Add butter and olive oil. Add onions and garlic and sauté until onions have browned, being careful not to burn the garlic. Add wine and Italian seasonings and deglaze the pan, about 2 to 3 minutes, until wine is reduced to a rich thick sauce. Stir in the cheese until melted. Cover to keep warm until burgers are ready. Serve burgers on warm buns with Dave's Famous Onion/ Blue Cheese topping.

WINE SUGGESTION:
Pick up a bottle of Truro Vineyards Cabernet Franc.

TWENTY-EIGHT ATLANTIC AT THE WEQUASSETT RESORT AND GOLF CLUB

2173 ROUTE 28
HARWICH, MA 02645
(508) 430-3000
WEQUASSETT.COM
EXECUTIVE CHEF: JAMES HACKNEY

If you're visiting the Cape and looking for an elegant dining experience, this special restaurant at the Wequassett Resort and Golf Club in Harwich is your place. The Wequassett Resort offers a bit of paradise, with twenty-seven acres of salt marshes and woodlands and breathtaking views of Pleasant Bay and the Atlantic Ocean. Executive Chef James Hackney, who hails from Leicestershire, England, says, "We want to offer a dining experience that parallels the luxury of Wequassett," and his food sure does that.

Chef Hackney began his culinary career by working in his parents' Garden Hotel, a quaint hotel in the English countryside, where farm-to-table was a way of life. And now, here on Cape Cod, he has cultivated relationships with local farmers, fishermen, and purveyors. Following his parents' example, he's using these local ingredients and putting his own creative twist on classic favorites. Try the Pleasant Bay Oysters, Atlantic Halibut, or the Butter Braised Lobster to see how Chef Hackney re-creates these Cape Cod favorites. The presentation is elegant and formal, as is the beautiful, spacious dining room. The waitstaff is attentive; everyone in the restaurant is there for you, making sure your experience is an exceptional one. Reservations are a must. Make sure to ask for a table by the window that faces the bay. If you time it right, you can add a spectacular sunset to what is sure to be an extraordinary meal.

CARAMELIZED SCALLOPS

(SERVES 4)

For the scallops:

2 pounds sea scallops, about 4 to 5 per person

For the pea puree:

2 pounds freshly shelled English peas, or best-quality frozen peas
2 tablespoons chopped fresh mint
1 cup water
1 tablespoon extra-virgin olive oil

For the carrot gnocchi:

½ pound carrots, peeled, trimmed, and cut into 2-inch chunks
5 tablespoons freshly grated Parmigiana Reggiano cheese, divided
3 tablespoons all-purpose flour
1 egg yolk
Pinch freshly grated nutmeg
Sea salt and freshly ground black pepper to taste

12 slices (about 6 ounces) prosciutto

To assemble the dish:

½ cup (4 ounces) unsalted butter
½ lemon for squeezing
Pea tendrils or mint sprigs for garnish

For the scallops: Rinse scallops in ice water and lay out on towels to air dry in refrigerator, 1 to 2 hours before searing. This will help with the searing process.

For the pea puree: Blanch fresh peas in boiling salted water for 3 minutes; drain well. Transfer peas to a blender and add the mint. With the blender running, slowly add the water to form a smooth puree; repeat with the olive oil. Transfer pea puree to an airtight container and refrigerate until ready to use. Rinse out the blender jar to use for the carrot gnocchi.

For the carrot gnocchi: Cook the carrots in boiling salted water until tender, about 10 to 12 minutes; drain well. Transfer carrots to the blender and puree until smooth. Add 3 tablespoons grated cheese, flour, egg yolk, nutmeg, and sea salt and freshly ground black pepper to taste; blend until evenly combined.

Scrape carrot dough into a piping bag fitted with a medium-size tip. Bring salted water to boil in a wide, shallow saucepan and have a bowl of ice water and a pair of clean kitchen scissors ready. Holding the piping bag over the saucepan, squeeze out the carrot dough and snip off 1-inch lengths so they drop into the boiling water. Boil until gnocchi rise to the surface, about 1 to 2 minutes, and use a slotted spoon to immediately transfer them to the ice bath; remove and pat dry. There should be about 20 gnocchi in all.

For the prosciutto: Preheat oven to 375°F. Line two rimmed baking sheets with parchment paper. Divide prosciutto slices between the baking sheets, laying them flat. Bake until fat turns golden and meat darkens, about 10 to 15 minutes.

To assemble the dish: Warm the pea puree in a small stainless steel saucepan over low heat, stirring often until heated through; set aside. Melt half the butter in a large sauté pan over high heat. Add the scallops and sear on both sides until caramelized on both sides, about 1 to 3 minutes per side. Transfer scallops to a plate. Wipe out the sauté pan and add the rest of the butter over high heat. Add the gnocchi and sauté, turning occasionally, until golden brown.

Dollop about 2 tablespoons warm pea puree in the middle of each of four dinner plates and use the back of a spoon to push the puree across the plate to create a design. Squeeze lemon juice over the scallops and gnocchi in the pan and then arrange them on top of the pea puree on each plate. Lean slices of crisp prosciutto against the scallops, trying not to cover the whole plate but giving it a nice design, then add pea tendrils or fresh mint as a garnish.

WINE SUGGESTION:
Premier Cru Chablis. Premier Cru Chablis is a gorgeous French white Burgundy which tends to exhibit bright floral and citrus flavors, with pure and vibrant minerality. It has the richness and weight to complement the scallops, while at the same time balancing the yummy goodness of the gnocchi and prosciutto.

Apple Tarte Tatin

(SERVES 4)

For the crust:

1 sheet puff pastry (half of a 17-ounce package), thawed but kept cold

For the tarte:

4–5 Granny Smith apples, peeled, cored, cut in half and quartered
5 tablespoons sugar, divided
1 teaspoon cinnamon
3 tablespoons water
3 tablespoon butter

For the honey cinnamon sour cream:

¾ cup sour cream
6 tablespoons honey
⅓ cup confectioner's sugar
¼ teaspoon ground cinnamon

For the crust: Unfold the pastry sheet on a lightly floured work surface. Invert a 6-inch-round cake pan on top of the dough and cut around it to form a circle of pastry slightly larger than the pan. Transfer the dough circle to a baking sheet and refrigerate until needed. Reserve the rest of the dough for another use.

For the tarte: Combine the apples, 1 tablespoon sugar, and cinnamon in a large bowl; toss to coat. Set aside.

Preheat oven 375°F. Put the remaining sugar and water into the bottom of a 6-inch cake pan and place over medium-high heat until the sugar turns golden brown. For a darker caramel, continue to cook but be careful not to burn the syrup. Stir in the butter until melted; tilt the pan to caramelize the sides. Use potholders to remove pan from heat.

Carefully position the apples flat side down (point side up) in a circle in the pan. Place the cake pan on a baking sheet for easier handling; bake until apples are just tender when poked with a paring knife, about 15 to 20 minutes. Remove apples from oven.

Place the cold puff pastry circle directly on top of the apples, tucking the edges down around the apples, and return to the oven. Bake until pastry is puffed, golden, and looks dry, about 20 minutes. Transfer tarte to a wire rack to cool slightly, 5 to 10 minutes.

Make sure that none of the pastry is stuck to the edges of the pan and invert a rimmed serving platter on top of the cake pan. Using potholders and working over the sink, hold the cake pan and platter firmly together and flip them so that the platter is on the bottom and the cake pan is on top. Set the whole thing down on the counter and carefully lift off the cake pan (juices will be hot). Replace any apples that stick to the skillet.

For the honey cinnamon sour cream: Combine sour cream, honey, sugar, and cinnamon in a bowl and mix well. Cover and refrigerate until serving time.

To assemble the dish: Using a long, sharp knife, cut the tarte into desired pieces and place a slice on each dessert plate. Pour a spoonful of the cream over each piece and serve immediately, while the apples are slightly warm.

Winslow's Tavern

316 Main Street
Wellfleet, MA 02667
(508) 349-6450
winslowstavern.com
General Manager: Tracy Barry Hunt
Chef: Phillip Hunt

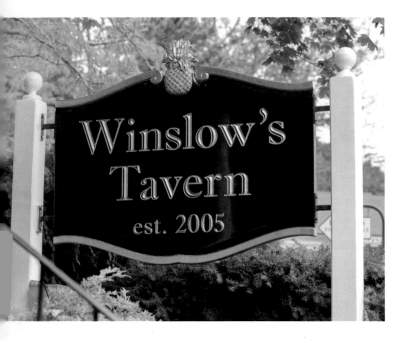

Tracy and Phillip Hunt have been running Winslow's Tavern since 2005. Tracy manages the front of the house, while Phillip runs the kitchen.

Phillip had moved from Johannesburg, South Africa, to New York City to pursue a career in fine art. Tracy was working in New York as a film producer. Their paths crossed while working on a documentary film, and they got married shortly after. They had shared a dream of opening a tapas bar in the city, but when Tracy's family, who already had a restaurant, decided to open another one in Wellfleet, their dream changed course. "Tracy's parents, who live in Wellfleet, told us about this tavern in the center of Wellfleet, and we jumped at it and here we are," says Phillip.

Phillip learned to cook from his mother, who owned several restaurants in Johannesburg. "I was a form of cheap labor and was dragged into the kitchen doing everything. I got to know fast what she expected of me in her kitchens," explains Phillip. Clearly those expectations were high. His use of local ingredients like Wellfleet oysters, Chatham cod, littleneck clams, monkfish, and mussels has made Winslow's Tavern one of the most popular restaurants on the Lower Cape.

The building that houses the restaurant has been a fixture in Wellfleet since 1805. Once a sea captain's house, in the 1920s it was the home of Massachusetts governor Channing Cox. Rumor has it that during this time President Calvin Coolidge was a guest. The building has been a restaurant for over forty years. Upgraded by its present owners, the tavern has a warm, open feel. If you're here on a warm summer night, make sure to ask to dine on the patio with its wonderful grape arbor.

GRILLED LOCAL SWORDFISH

(SERVES 4)

For the pan tomatoes:

2 teaspoons extra-virgin olive oil

1 teaspoon minced shallots

1 teaspoon minced garlic

1 teaspoon crushed red pepper flakes

½ cup Nicoise olives, pitted and halved

¼ cup large capers, drained

1 cup white wine

4 vine ripe tomatoes, cut into ¾-inch cubes

1 teaspoon sugar

½ cup packed fresh parsley leaves

1 teaspoon grated fresh lemon zest

Salt and pepper to taste

For the pan swordfish:

2 teaspoons olive oil

Salt and pepper to taste

4 (10-ounce) swordfish fillets

For the romaine hearts:

2 teaspoons extra-virgin olive oil

Salt and pepper to taste

2 romaine hearts, halved lengthwise

For the pan tomatoes: Heat the oil in a large sauté pan over low heat. Add the shallots, garlic, and red pepper flakes and cook slowly just until shallots are translucent but not brown, about 10 minutes. Add the olives and capers, stirring to coat. Raise the heat to high, and when it is sizzling hot, add the wine. Cook, stirring, until most of the wine has evaporated, about 6 to 8 minutes more. Add the tomatoes and sugar and toss until the tomatoes just start to collapse. Stir in the parsley leaves and lemon zest and season to taste with salt and pepper. Set aside.

For the swordfish: Oil and season the swordfish and place over a medium-hot fire until opaque all the way through, about 4 minutes per side.

For the romaine hearts: While the fish is cooking, heat the oil in a large sauté pan over medium heat. Season the romaine hearts with salt and pepper and arrange them cut sides down in the oil. Cook until golden brown on all sides, turning carefully with tongs to keep the leaves neatly together.

To assemble the dish: Gently reheat the tomatoes. Arrange the romaine hearts on four serving plates, one half for each serving, fanning out the leaves. Place a swordfish fillet on top of the romaine and divide the tomatoes over the fish. Lightly drizzle with a quality extra-virgin olive oil and serve immediately.

WINE SUGGESTION:
Arneis. Arneis is a full-bodied Italian white wine from Piedmont with elegant flavors of apricot, peach, and white pepper, along with moderate acidity and a spicy finish which pairs nicely with the bold flavors accompanying the grilled swordfish.

Recipe Index

General Index

PHOTO BY DEB JOHNSON

About the Author

John F. Carafoli is an internationally known food stylist, consultant, and food writer. He wrote the seminal book *Food Photography and Styling* and two children's cookbooks, *Look Who's Cooking* and *The Cookie Cookbook*. He has been published in the *New York Times* and *Gastronomica*. In addition to presenting papers at the prestigious Oxford Symposium on Food and Cookery in England, he organized the biannual International Conference on Food Styling and Photography at Boston University.

Carafoli is currently working on a historical, American-Italian emergent cookbook. He has written a quarterly feature "In Carafoli's Kitchen" for the magazine *Edible Cape Cod,* and won an Eddy award for the best use of recipes in an article. Carafoli has also been featured on the Food Network and NPR. For further updates and information about the restaurants visit his blog at carafoli.com.

About the Photographer

Francine Zaslow has been creating beautiful images professionally for over two decades. After graduating from the University of the Arts in Philadelphia, she settled in Boston, where she built a diverse client base including Panera Bread, Fage, Au Bon Pain, Whole Foods, Fresh, Bose, Timberland, New Balance, and Mariposa.

Zaslow has won awards from *Communication Arts, Photo District News,* Big Picture Show, Saint Botolphs Society, and Hasselblad.

As an artist, Zaslow has always believed that inspiration comes from the unexpected. Reaching into the far corners of life's experiences, she has created a diverse collection of personal images.

Zaslow is both the photographer and the director, manipulating light, sculpting forms, and transforming her subjects with a deliberate eye.

You can view her photographs at francinezaslow.com.

© ADAM DETOUR